DR. MARTHA HUGHES CANNON

Martha Hughes Cannon

DR. MARTHA HUGHES CANNON

SUFFRAGIST, SENATOR, PLURAL WIFE

CONSTANCE L. LIEBER

SIGNATURE BOOKS | 2022 | SALT LAKE CITY

The opinions expressed in this book are not necessarily those of the publisher.

Design by Jason Francis.

FIRST EDITION | 2022

LIBRARY OF CONGRESS CONTROL NUMBER: 2022943827

Paperback ISBN: 978-1-56085-457-9
Ebook ISBN: 978-1-56085-433-3

It is the biographer's joy,
as she considers someone else's path,
to find her own life transformed.
Thank you, Mattie.
You have transformed mine.

CONTENTS

PREFACE AND ACKNOWLEDGMENTS

I discovered Mattie Cannon by accident. As an archivist for the Church of Jesus Christ of Latter-day Saints, I was going through boxes and boxes of uncatalogued letters and manuscripts. I opened the boxes marked "Maria Munn" and stared at the letter I had just carefully removed from its box:

> Apr 20, [18]86
> Dear Munn: —
> "The gallant ship is under weigh
> To bear us off to sea.
> And yonder floats the streamers gay
> That says she waits for 'we'
> The seamen dip the ready oar
> As rippling waves oft tell
> They bear us swiftly from the shore
> Our native land farewell."
> "Everything is lovely, and the goose hangs high."
> Sweet Elizabeth has not even got the "snuffles", and now lies rolling on the floor, has kicked off her stockings and is licking your photo. The way she crowed when I gave it her, I do believe she thought it had some connection with her pa. Have had a splendid time—now I must put on babe's things and off we go.[1]

But something was not quite right about this group of letters. As I skimmed them, phrases jumped out at me:

---

1. Constance L. Lieber and John Sillito, eds., *Letters From Exile: The Correspondence of Martha Hughes Cannon and Angus M. Cannon, 1886–1888* (Salt Lake City: Signature Books, 1989), 5. Unless noted, all excerpts from the correspondence of Martha Hughes Cannon and Angus M. Cannon are taken from this book. The originals are in Church History Library, Church of Jesus Christ of Latter-day Saints, Salt Lake City.

[May 4, 1886]: I have told my relatives that I married a widower.[2]

[May 20, 1886]: My Dear Husband: — There! Now I hear you ejaculate, that is a very "<u>uncautious</u>" heading for these perilous times.[3]

[July 9, 1886]: You speak of me "giving up all for you." Has it ever occurred to you how much you have given up for me?[4]

[January 3, 1887]: [My uncle] became furious, saying I was "not an honored wife," but connected with one of those things out there! Etc., etc. I suppose one of "those things" meant you.[5]

Maria was clearly an educated and literate woman. Her letters are strewn with quotations: from *Les Miserables* and *Hamlet*; from Robert Burns and Henry Wadsworth Longfellow; Aldous Huxley and Hubert Howe Bancroft. She refers to her "profession" and states that the more she is allowed to move about freely, as men can, the happier she is.

And almost every letter ends with the exhortation to "Munn" to "be sure and burn every line of this!"[6]

I was convinced now that her name was *not* "Maria Munn," as she was so clearly concerned with concealing her identity.

A rather cryptic letter dated December 13, 1886, addressed to "Bro. Mac" and signed "Ezekiel Brown," furnished more clues. The author (although signed "Ezekiel Brown," it is clearly still "Maria" writing) refers to an article in the *Salt Lake Herald* of November 25, 1886:

> I shall not attempt to describe my feelings upon reading of the arrest of our mutual friend Bro. Angus ... "Cohabitation," in this case I think [is] simply a bait at which Dickson would like Cannon to bite, and while he is doing penance for his indulgence, the former gent expects to see little Hughes go flying home to her nest, when he will set his will to grinding again, and present "Polygamy" or "Perjury", Sir Angus & lady Mattie —as you prefer. Proud Angus would not let one of the fair sex suffer ignominy for his sake, and so they have him for a long period— god forbid!!

---

2. Lieber and Sillito, *Letters From Exile*, 8.
3. Lieber and Sillito, *Letters from Exile.*
4. Lieber and Sillito, *Letters From Exile*, 22.
5. Lieber and Sillito, *Letters From Exile*, 84–85.
6. Lieber and Sillito, *Letters From Exile*, 87.

Clearly "Maria" is a polygamous wife of "Munn." The year 1886 was the height of the polygamy persecutions in Utah, and William H. Dickson was the district attorney for the Territory of Utah who figured prominently in the arrests of fugitive polygamists. This letter also provides three additional names: Cannon, Mattie, and Angus. Could these be the real names of our correspondents?

I consulted *The Latter-day Saint Biographical Encyclopedia* by Andrew Jenson. In volume 1 was the following entry: "Cannon, Angus Munn, president of the Salt Lake Stake of Zion since 1876." It went on to name his wives: Sarah Maria and Ann Amanda Mousley, Clarissa Cordelia Moses, and—there she was, my cryptic "Maria"— Martha (Mattie) Hughes, wife number four.[7]

An entry for Martha Hughes Cannon was in volume 4: "Born on 1 Jul 1857 in Llandudno, Wales. Went to medical school at the University of Michigan and the University of Pennsylvania. Resident physician at the Deseret Hospital in Salt Lake City. Married Angus M. Cannon on 6 October 1884."[8]

Angus M. Cannon was an important and influential man in late nineteenth-century Utah. He was the president of the Salt Lake Stake of the Church of Jesus Christ of Latter-day Saints, which comprised some 50,000 members in what are now four states (all of Utah and parts of Idaho, Nevada, and Arizona). His powerful older brother, George Q. Cannon, was a counselor to church presidents John Taylor (the successor to Brigham Young), Wilford Woodruff, and Lorenzo Snow. As such, Angus should figure prominently in the history books.

He didn't figure at all.

His wife, Martha—or "Mattie," as she was commonly known— was a physician, the mother of three children, an advocate for woman's rights. Remarkably, she was elected as the first-ever female state senator in 1896 in an at-large election in which her husband also ran—and lost. She sponsored many important bills, including one to

7. Andrew Jenson, *Latter-day Saint Biographical Encyclopedia: A Compilation of Biographical Sketches of Prominent Men and Women in the Church of Jesus Christ of Latter-day Saints*, 4 vols. (Salt Lake City: The Andrew Jenson History Company, 1901–36), 1:292–95.

8. Jenson, *Latter-day Saint Biographical Encyclopedia*, 4:86–88.

establish Utah's State Board of Health. Her accomplishments were noteworthy and groundbreaking. She had earned her place in history.

Yet she had faded into obscurity and merited barely a footnote in most histories.

Since that long-ago day in the Church Archives (now the Church History Library), I have devoted myself to learning about this woman. I wanted to understand why (in 1976) apparently no one knew of her and why the history books ignored her. I wanted to understand why her oldest granddaughter did not find out until she read it in Mattie's obituary that her grandmother had been a senator. I wanted to understand what compelled Mattie to protect her privacy so completely that she requested her son burn all her journals and papers after her death. (Sadly, he did.) Why was a woman who figured so largely in late nineteenth-century Utah public life largely ignored in the journals and writings of her contemporaries? And what, if anything, did she have to say to us today?

I puzzled over these and similar questions for years, and like all long friendships, ours was fraught with ups and downs. A decade would pass, and I would neglect her. I was tired of her whining, her hypochondria, her depressions. Her difficulties and the way she engaged with life echoed much of what was happening in my own, and I needed all my emotional energies to deal with that instead of a long-dead woman who had inserted herself into my mental space. I identified with her; I withdrew from her. Is that, perhaps, what had happened with some of her contemporaries?

Then, in 2011, Nancy Green, a producer at KUED television at the University of Utah in Salt Lake City, contacted me about a documentary she was preparing on the life of Martha Hughes Cannon. So I dusted off my boxes of research, tried to decipher cryptic notes that must have meant something to me twenty years earlier, and worked with Nancy to resurrect a nearly forgotten historical figure.

This short biography is a labor of love. Because her personal papers were not extant, I traced Mattie's steps from Wales to Salt Lake City, Michigan, Philadelphia, Europe, and, finally, California, where she died in 1932.

Retracing Mattie's steps took me from Utah to Philadelphia; Algonac and Ann Arbor, Michigan; Warwickshire and London,

England; and Basel and Bern, Switzerland. In all those places many people helped me find my way to Mattie:

Mrs. Joan M. Bullen, of the Algonac/Clay Historical Society, who graciously opened the officially closed building when I arrived. We were both excited to realize that that building—the Bostwick Building—was where Dr. W. K. Moore, who assisted Mattie when she operated on Emily Stomlar, had his offices in 1881 when Mattie was there.

Sibyl Moses, at the Library of Congress, who was so excited when we finally found mention of Mattie in their records, that she (and I) gave out a whoop and were promptly shushed.

Annie Tucker, of Warner Coaching, who patiently corrected my thought processes, made sure that people besides me could understand the nascent manuscript, and wouldn't let me slack off.

The expert curator of the Susan B. Anthony papers at the Library of Congress, who, though she couldn't let me handle the fragile papers myself, used her own time to check if there was any mention of Mattie in them. (There wasn't.)

The young woman who rented the Paul family home on 900 East in Salt Lake City before it was torn down and showed me all over the house and garden, afterward posting photos of Mattie and Angus in her kitchen.

The members of the Cannon family: JoAnn Peterson, who gave me my first personal look at Mattie as her family knew her; Arline Brady, who welcomed me into her home and showed me photographs and the Senate autograph book and shared her memories; Helen Ovard, Mattie's oldest grandchild, who shared memories of her grandmother. Most especially Blaine Brady, Mattie's first great-great-grandchild, who shared his vast knowledge of his great-great-grandmother, patiently answering question after question, and (to my great delight) telling me that I "was family," too.

My husband, Wilford Lieber, who read draft after draft, never complaining, giving me excellent feedback, and accompanying me to Michigan and England to trace Mattie's path.

The Reverend John Nightengale, of Wolverton, England, who took my friend Beatrice and me all around the countryside in his car until we located the former cottage of Joseph Twyman. He also arranged for me to be interviewed on a local radio station. The interviewer was astounded and nearly speechless to learn that there had been Mormon plural wives in Wolverton and Norton Lindsey in 1886.

To Nancy Green of KUED, the producer of the documentary on Mattie, thank you for reawakening my interest and encouraging me to finish the journey of recording Mattie's life.

To so many who allowed themselves to be interviewed and graciously answered my questions: D. Michael Quinn, Jill Mulvay Derr, Cherry Silver, and Lisa Tait. There are undoubtedly others: your input was just as invaluable.

CHAPTER ONE

FROM WALES TO UTAH

The Hughes family were poor, lower-class members of Llandudno (Wales) society. However, Mattie's mother, Elizabeth Evans, had come from a higher social class, which the family did not forget (nor did she let them forget) and which lent them a certain cachet among themselves and among their relatives. Evans apparently had a certain haughtiness in her manner: a *soupçon* of superiority. Her daughter seems to have inherited a measure of this. Photographs show that both wore round, rimless eyeglasses and had the same strong chin. However, Evans was "a large woman, a good housekeeper and a good cook,"[1] while, by all accounts, her petite daughter was neither a good housekeeper nor a good cook—Mattie hired girls to do that for her later in life.

Mattie's mother came from Warwickshire where she worked for a titled lady (likely picking up some of the habits and mannerisms of that class) and where she learned to do fine needlework. Later she was employed as a chambermaid at a hotel in Llandudno where she met Peter Hughes. Evans's biographer, Mattie's daughter Elizabeth Rachel, describes Llandudno as being "at the west end of the crescent bay of Llandudno, a beautiful watering place in northern Wales" marked by the Great Orme, a prominent limestone headland.[2] It was not a large town—by 1847, the population was only around 1,000. It was specifically built as a Victorian holiday resort. Most of the men were employed as copper miners, fishermen, and subsistence farmers. Hughes was a cabinetmaker employed in repairing and restoring

---

1. Elizabeth Cannon McCrimmon, "Grandma Paul," Mar. 1968, 1, copy in my possession.
2. McCrimmon, "Grandma Paul," 2.

1

the interior woodwork of several crumbling castles in Wales. Evans had well-to-do parents (at least compared to the Hughes family) who objected to Peter because he was below her class. Nonetheless, they married on February 4, 1854.

Elizabeth and Peter Hughes were early converts to the Church of Jesus Christ of Latter-day Saints. What was important to Mattie, from her childhood until her death, was that her parents were faithful Mormons and that she was determined to follow their example. Even in the midst of her exile, prompted by US government persecution of polygamists, she stood firm.

Joining the LDS Church was not an easy endeavor in 1850 Wales—or anywhere else, for that matter. Elizabeth Evans's sister-in-law, Catherine Hughes Roberts, was a convert, baptized on August 5, 1850. Catherine, in turn, converted Elizabeth and her husband Peter—to the horror of Elizabeth's mother who had heard many lurid tales of life among the Mormons in Utah, especially tales of young women being forced to marry into polygamy.[3] She was devastated when she learned that the family planned to go to Utah. "You may go yourself," she declared. "That we cannot prevent. But you shall not take the children. The law will justify and help us there, and we shall surely invoke it. … So the young couple gathered up what belongings they could not dispose of and … stole away."[4]

Peter and Elizabeth had managed to scrape together enough money to pay their passage to New York City on the *Underwriter*, a schooner that had carried Mormon converts on earlier voyages from Liverpool to New York. According to the records of the church's British Mission office in Liverpool, "Peter Hughes, a joiner aged 35 from Tanygraig, Wales, together with his wife Elizabeth, 27, from Llandudno, Carnarvon, Wales and their young daughters, Mary E., 5; Martha M., 2; and Anne (infant)" paid a total of 15 pounds, 8 shillings, 8 pence" for their fares.[5]

On March 30, 1860, the *Underwriter* sailed from Liverpool, England, and arrived at New York City on May 1. The emigrants who

---

3. John Henry Evans, "Martha Hughes Cannon," *Relief Society Magazine* 19, no. 10 (Oct. 1932): 584.

4. Evans, "Martha Hughes Cannon," 586.

5. Emigration Records of the Liverpool Office, British Mission, p. 146, CR 271 25, Church History Library, Church of Jesus Christ of Latter-day Saints, Salt Lake City.

could afford the journey continued on to Florence, Nebraska. Once there, LDS emigration agents helped them outfit themselves for the long trek to Utah.[6]

The family stories, as told by Mattie's daughter Elizabeth Rachel and her half-sister Maude Paul, both illuminate and complicate the historical record. Official records do not reconcile totally with family reminiscences, which is not uncommon. Life begins at birth—usually a definitively recorded date, but after that, the stories take over, with ever-widening circles of influence overcoming the storytellers, who then tell an amended version of events. In the Hughes family, Elizabeth Rachel (Mattie's daughter) is the storyteller, the one determined to make sure her mother's story would always be heard. Her early writings are clearer, truer. Her accuracy waned as she aged, and she found herself relying on a failing memory as she wrote about her mother's legacy.

By the time they arrived in New York, the family's funds were exhausted. Unable to afford the journey westward, they remained stranded with hundreds of other destitute European church members, scattered in East Coast cities from Boston to Philadelphia.

Peter Hughes was ill; Elizabeth tended their three daughters and sewed men's ties for a large clothing establishment. She earned money for rent and food by nursing and taking in washing.

Elizabeth Rachel recorded that one day Erastus Snow, a high-ranking apostle of the Church of Jesus Christ of Latter-day Saints, visited the Hughes family. He had been appointed to go to New York City and its neighbors and neighboring states to gather together stranded members, get them to Winter Quarters, Nebraska, and organize immigrant companies so they could make the trek to Zion (Utah). He gave the Hughes family four dollars to help them get to the staging point in Florence, Nebraska. "[There] he obtained ½ wagon for them to occupy while crossing the plains."[7]

---

6. "Sailing Vessels and Steamboats," in Kate B. Carter, *Our Pioneer Heritage*, vol. 12 (Salt Lake City: Daughters of Utah Pioneers, 1958), 421–92. This article has an introduction followed by a year-by-year summary of each ship used for emigration. Some entries have accounts from *Church Chronology* by Andrew Jenson, from the *Latter-day Saints' Millennial Star*, or the *Times and Seasons*. Pictures of the *Underwriter* are accessible online.

7. McCrimmon, "Grandma Paul," 1.

Brigham Young had called several men experienced in crossing the plains to go to Florence, Nebraska, and bring the poor European Saints to Zion,[8] all part of a meticulously planned project. Similar to previous emigrant groups, they "traveled in semi-military fashion, grouped into companies of 100s, 50s and 10s. Discipline, hard work, mutual assistance, and devotional practices were part of their daily routine."[9] On their way east, each team carried a supply of food for themselves and their teams, plus cornmeal to trade with the native Indians. Some of the provisions were left at designated waystations to be picked up by later emigrant companies since wagons loaded with emigrants and their few possessions could not carry sufficient supplies for the journey to Utah.[10]

The Hughes family traveled with the Joseph Horne Company, one of several emigrant companies leaving at the same time, as groups led by Ira Eldredge, John Murdock, and Milo Andrus. The Horne Company left from the outfitting post at Florence, Nebraska, in early July 1861, arriving in Salt Lake City on September 13.

By 1861, the arrival of emigrants was a continual occurrence and therefore no longer news. As the church-owned *Deseret News* reflected in a September 11, 1861, article:

Companies of the immigrating Saints have been arriving at short intervals for some days as we are informed, but their arrival has attracted so little attention that our local reporter has not been particularly interested in the matter, at least if he has made himself acquainted with the facts he has not made report, and we have had so many other matters to see after during the last two weeks, that we have not had time nor opportunity to make the necessary enquiries to ascertain whether one, two, three, four or more companies have come in … but we are of [the] opinion that a majority of the independent companies have arrived, and that the others will be here shortly.[11]

8. James Olsen, "Autobiographical sketch," 1921, 4–5, Joseph Horne Company, at history.lds.org/overlandtravels. This LDS Church History Library project documented personal narratives excerpted from journals and reminiscences by participants on the trek to Utah. The Hughes family, as far as is known, left no record behind, so we can only surmise their travels from the stories of others.

9. *Mormon Pioneer Trail* (Washington, DC: National Park Service, n.d.).

10. William John Hill, [Autobiography], in *Utah Pioneer Biographies*, 32:85, in *Overland Trail Database, 1847–1868*, history.lds.org/overlandtravels.

11. "The Immigaation [sic]," *Deseret News*, Sep. 11, 1861.

The plains were busy in 1861, and the several companies of emigrants bound for Utah were not the only ones heading west. The Hughes family doubtless had contact with the other church emigrant companies, crossing and overtaking each other repeatedly. As they were often within visual distance of each other, there was apparently a bit of competition to be the leading company. At least one member of the Murdock Company was "mortified" to have to allow the Horne Company to overtake them at one point.[12]

As they plodded along, they would have seen men laying lines for the first transcontinental telegraph, as well as overland stagecoaches and Pony Express riders speeding past them, lending some excitement to their day.[13] They passed existing settlements and the occasional lone cabin and had several peaceful encounters with the Sioux and Pawnee Indians.

In addition to the minimal risk of attack by Indians, the emigrants faced possible accidental injury and death. Falling underneath the wagon wheels, easily done when climbing in and out of the wagon, was one of the most frequent causes of death. Exposure, exhaustion, firearm accidents, disease, and lightning were other dangers. Mattie, although only five years old, noticed much of this, including the hasty burial of infants and the grief of their mothers. Her anxiety would have been deepened by her father's fragile state. These remembered snapshots of death and suffering remained with her over ten years later when she began working, saving, and studying to become a physician.

Peter was sick the entire trip and rode in the half of a wagon assigned to the Hughes family. Mattie and her sister Mary Elizabeth, by now seven and five years old, and the even younger Annie, would also have ridden much of the time. Elizabeth, however, walked the whole way, wearing out all of her shoes and finishing the trek with her feet wrapped in rags.

---

12. Frederick W. Blake, Diary, Apr.–Dec. 30, 1861, in Ira Eldredge Company, *Overland Trail Database*, history.lds.org/overlandtravels.

13. Mary Ann Hafen, *Recollections of a Handcart Pioneer of 1860: A Woman's Life on the Mormon Frontier* (N.p.: by the author, 1938), 21–26.

CHAPTER TWO

EARLY DAYS IN UTAH

The Horne Company made their first Utah Territory camp in Green River, located in today's Wyoming. They then traveled about ninety more miles and camped at Yellow Creek, near present-day Evanston. The next day, September 8, they began traveling down Echo Canyon and arrived in today's state of Utah. They celebrated their arrival by holding a dance. But the Hughes family did not celebrate with them: it was the day they buried one-year-old Annie Lloyd.

Later, Elizabeth Rachel recorded the death: "Little Annie succumbed to the hardships and was buried along the roadside. The family covered the shallow grave with rocks in order to keep the wild animals from disturbing the small body."[1] According to Elizabeth, Mattie's memory of her young sister being lowered into a grave (that had to be immediately abandoned as the wagons rolled westward) stayed with her, and she recalled over and over through the years just how helpless they all had been to prevent such deaths and avoid such sorrow.[2]

The morning of September 11 was cold and frosty. The emigrants crossed East Canyon Creek half a dozen times before they started ascending Big Mountain from whose summit they had their first view of the Salt Lake Valley.

The rest of that day and most of the next were spent on church business. One by one, the head of each family was called to a tent where they gave their emigration notes to church agents, signing their agreement to gradually repay their share of the cost of the trek.

1. Elizabeth C. McCrimmon, "Dr. Martha Hughes Cannon, First Woman State Senator in America," Utah State Historical Society, Salt Lake City.

2. Elizabeth C. McCrimmon, "Dr. Martha Hughes Cannon, First Woman State Senator in America," *Seydell Quarterly* 11, no. 2 (Winter 1959): 6.

Probably Elizabeth Evans took care of that instead of Peter Hughes. Gravely ill, he would die only a few days after they reached the city.

Late in the afternoon of September 12 they broke camp and crossed Little Mountain. Their trail led to the bottom of the canyon (now under Little Dell Reservoir), and, there being no switchbacks to ease their climb, the pioneers hitched multiple teams of stock together to pull the wagons straight up the slope. Once at the top, they locked the wheels and slid straight down the other side into Emigration Canyon where they camped for the last time before finally entering Salt Lake Valley.

Mattie and Mary Elizabeth were certainly among the children who, "all cleaned up," ran ahead of the train on September 13, eager to enter the Salt Lake Valley at last.[3] As was usual, the train made its final stop at the Eighth Ward Public Square, site of today's elaborate Romanesque-style City–County Building.[4] The long journey was over.

Elizabeth Rachel described the Hughes family's arrival in Salt Lake City. Peter Hughes was buried in a grave site situated in a gully in the Salt Lake City Cemetery. Mattie's only recollection of her father was his tall, dark figure in his coffin.[5]

Elizabeth Hughes was given the decrepit wagon, which she rolled up against a bluff on the acre and a quarter she and her two daughters were allotted on the eastern bench of the city at today's 537 South 900 East. Behind the wagon, she scooped out a cave to use as a kitchen. The family slept in the wagon. To earn money, she took in her neighbors' washing.[6]

---

3. Sarah Bethula Palmer Sharp, "Autobiographical sketch," 1931, at history.lds.org/overlandtravel.

4. Descriptions of the emigrant trail in Utah as it was and as it appears today are taken from personal observation and from the following informational brochures: *Mormon Pioneer Trail* and *Mormon Pioneer National Historic Trail* (Washington, DC: National Park Service, n.d.); *The Mormon Trail: Fort Bridger to Salt Lake City* (Salt Lake City: Utah Historic Trails Consortium, n.d.); *Lincoln Highway: The Main Street Across America, Driving Guide* (N.p.: Summit County Historical Society, 2008); *Echo Canyon Driving Guide* (N.p: Summit County Historical Society, 2000); *National Historic Trails Auto Tour Route Interpretive Guide: Utah—Crossroads of the West* (Washington, DC: National Park Service, Sep. 2010).

5. Elizabeth C. McCrimmon to Claire Noall, Feb. 13, 1938, Special Collections, J. Willard Marriott Library, University of Utah, Salt Lake City.

6. McCrimmon to Noall, Feb. 13, 1938.

Elizabeth's youngest daughter, Maude Paul, describes a life that was not easy. "To win their bread and clothing was no light task, since everything that could not be raised or crudely made had to be brought a thousand miles by ox teams. Sugar cane was made into molasses, which was used in the place of sugar. A twisted rag drawn through a button placed in a saucer of grease served for a light, and every other necessity was correspondingly crude."[7] And it was winter, which in Salt Lake City means bitter cold and much snow.

Life looked more hopeful after Elizabeth married James Patton Paul, a widower with four children, on October 25, 1862, just over a year after the Hughes family arrived in Salt Lake City. She brought her two surviving daughters into the family with Paul and his four children—two girls and two boys by his first wife, Robina Gibben. They built a small adobe home on Elizabeth's land. Five additional children were born to Elizabeth and James Paul, resulting in a large, sometimes rambunctious family. Mattie later recalled her parents telling each other: "Your children and my children are abusing our children."[8]

Life was not just about earning a living. Maude recalled her father and mother walking about one and a half miles every Sunday afternoon to the Tabernacle in downtown Salt Lake City for afternoon church services. Attending church on Sundays and participating in other weekday religious activities was the constant backdrop of their existence—and something that defined Mattie and her approach to meeting life's challenges.

Maude's description of her parents points out other traits Mattie had in common with them: "Father [James] was of medium height and slender build, but because of his erect carriage and the high silk stove pipe hat worn at that time, he looked much taller. For dress occasions, with his black suit, white shirt and vests of white and buff-colored material embroidered with tiny flowers and carrying a cane," he looked very elegant. Elizabeth "had masses of wavy gold-brown hair that reached her waist. She wore it in coronet style braided on top of her head while the back part hung in ringlets

<hr>

7. Sarah Maud Paul, "Sketch of the Life of Elizabeth Hughes Paul, A Utah Pioneer of 1862 [1861] Prepared by Her Daughter, Maude Paul," copy in my possession
8. McCrimmon, "Dr. Martha Hughes Cannon," *Seydell Quarterly*, 3.

over her shoulders, fastened by a comb. She always wore feather or flower-trimmed bonnets with wide ribbon bows tied at one side. A shawl of silk or paisley was also worn, as was the fashion."[9]

Looking fashionable—a way of implying a more elevated up-bringing than one might suppose of the wife of a carpenter—was obviously important to Elizabeth and James, and to Mattie as well. However, Mattie also learned that her mother was able to sacrifice her precious clothing when more important things could be done with the money. It was a lesson Mattie practiced during her years at medical school when her clothes, by her own admission, had gotten quite shabby.

Mattie was growing up and beginning to broaden her horizons beyond her immediate family, interacting more with others in her community. Sometime around her fourteenth birthday, in 1871, she began a very short career teaching school. She taught at an "infant school," but three pupils—the "three Jims"—were bigger than she was and caused too much trouble. She gave up teaching rather quickly.[10] About this time, she would have left behind her girlhood wardrobe and donned adult clothing. Until then, she probably wore her hair long and loose along with dresses shorter than ankle length. But now, combs, hairpins, hair lying heavy on the head, and long skirts were new to her—and probably unwelcome.

Mattie never wrote a description of this change in her life, but her daughter passed down stories of Mattie defying societal strictures of female attire—refusing at least part of that martyrdom by wearing shorter skirts and men's boots and by cutting off her hair for practical reasons. Mattie simply chose to wear clothes that made life easier.

She worked hard to earn the money she would eventually need to go east to study medicine. Among other things, she learned to set type for the *Deseret News*, the *Woman's Exponent*, and several Scandinavian-language newspapers.

While growing to adulthood, Mattie would have seen her mother and other women go to the voting polls to exercise their right, which Utah women gained in 1870. Mattie's civic education was enhanced

9. Paul, "Sketch of the Life of Elizabeth Hughes Paul."
10. McCrimmon to Noall, Feb. 13, 1938.

by her growing acquaintance with Emmeline B. Wells, who, through her editorship of the *Woman's Exponent*, kept Utah women informed of the political and civic issues that concerned them. It was in the *Woman's Exponent* that Mattie published the minutes of the Tenth Ward Young Women's Retrenchment Association (on 410 South 800 East near her home), where Mattie served as secretary beginning at age thirteen.

However, she did not limit herself simply to nóting what had happened and who spoke on what subject. She inserted her own commentary on the lessons and talks she heard and included several poems (she termed them "essays") that she wrote herself. As a result of her detailed minutes, we can get a fair idea of her religious education—which, in the 1870s, was the same as her civic education.

Mattie was, at first, an assistant secretary, and her sister Mary a counselor in the Retrenchment Association. By the spring of 1873, Mattie had been promoted to secretary. The way she signed the minutes she submitted to the ward shows that she was struggling with the issue of what to name herself. Hughes, after her father? Paul after the stepfather she loved? Or a combination? At various times she used the following names: M. H. Paul, M. M. Paul, M. Hughes Paul, Mattie Hughes Paul, Mattie H. Paul, Mattie Paul, and M. Maria H. Paul. It was not until she returned to Utah from her medical studies in 1884 that she was finally known as Mattie Paul Hughes, and then, after her marriage, as Martha Hughes Cannon. But always everyone called her simply "Mattie."[11]

During Retrenchment Association meetings, Mattie began acquiring skills that became important to her future professional life. In an August 5, 1873, meeting of the association, the girls were encouraged to not be timid in speaking. Miss A. Graham stated (in Mattie's words) that "she felt great good would result from the little meetings which were held by the young ladies; they were thus preparing themselves for future usefulness."[12] A prescient statement, given the trajectory of Mattie's life.

Another lesson Mattie learned at these meetings led to her eventual determination to accept Mormon polygamy so she could marry

11. The exception was Angus, Mattie's husband, who always called her "Martha."
12. "R.S. Reports," *Woman's Exponent*, Oct. 1, 1873.

a good man within the church—with emphasis on his spirituality and not "someone [merely] left over after the others girls had had their pick."[13] Mattie records the following personal thought in her minutes for August 19, 1873: "[It is] extremely distressing to see beautiful young women marrying gentiles for they are left, with a very few exceptions discarded women, [and] often die away from their friends at home. Let us be prayerful and prepare ourselves to battle all outside influences and temptations."[14]

Mattie absorbed the talks given by prominent women such as Emmeline B. Wells and Eliza R. Snow, who spoke out for women's rights in a way that must have seemed daring, if not radical, at the time. Still, as the following statement by Eliza Snow shows, it was done in a way that still echoed the Victorian image of a worthy woman: "[We are] women who stand not as dictators, but as counselors to their husbands, and who, in the purest, noblest sense of refined womanhood, are truly helpmates—we not only speak because we have the right, but justice and humanity demand that we should."[15]

Mattie's daughter Elizabeth Rachel said that her grandparents, assuming Mattie's "older, taller, and stronger" sister, Mary, was destined to study medicine, had purchased medical books for her. But Mary, "engrossed in parties," was not interested, so Mattie purchased them from her and began reading them at night. "Mother hated poverty, loved anything 'swell'—it was that combined with a desire to bring modern science to suffering pioneer women that made her determined to study medicine: relief for suffering women; relief from poverty."[16]

In 1876 Mattie, now nineteen, was a year into her study of chemistry at the University of Deseret (now the University of Utah). On June 7, 1878, she was awarded a "certificate" from the academic department, having "completed the Course of Study in Chemistry."[17]

13. "Our Woman Senator. The First to Be Elected in America: Mrs. Cannon Interviewed," *Salt Lake Herald*, Nov. 11, 1896.

14. Tenth Ward Young Women's Mutual Improvement Association, 1870–73, Tenth Ward, Park Stake, LR 9051 17, Church History Library, Church of Jesus Christ of Latter-day Saints, Salt Lake City.

15. Edward W. Tullidge, *Women of Mormondom* (New York: Tullidge & Crandall, 1877), 392.

16. McCrimmon to Noall, Feb. 13, 1938.

17. "Home Affairs," *Woman's Exponent*, June 15, 1878.

Mattie did what she could to prepare to enter the University of Michigan the next fall. The *Exponent* praised her efforts: "Miss Paul has been qualifying herself for some time past in the study of medicine and surgery, preparatory to going East with the intention of perfecting herself in these attainments. She has educated herself by her own energy, industry and economy and earned money to defray her college expenses; and her example of diligence and perseverance is worthy of imitation. Miss Paul is a young lady of exceptional ability and deserves to succeed."[18]

The final step of her preparation was to be set apart—invoking the blessings of God and demonstrating the support of church leaders—to study medicine in the East. To that end Mattie and three other women met church president John Taylor and one of his counselors, George Q. Cannon (brother of Mattie's future husband), in the Church Historian's Office on August 11, 1878. The other women were Romania B. Pratt and Ellis R. Shipp, who had recently graduated from medical school, and Maggie Shipp, who was going to study at the Women's Medical College in Philadelphia. Romania and Maggie were set apart by Taylor; Ellis and Mattie by Cannon. The other three women were already married and had children. Mattie represented the rising generation.[19]

The next four years would take Mattie from the relatively small community of Salt Lake City to the larger city of Ann Arbor, Michigan, and later to even larger Philadelphia, where she received diplomas from both the University of Pennsylvania and the National School of Elocution and Oratory. These years would be informed by three tensions that would challenge the world she grew up in: (1) the struggle to prove herself as a female in an environment populated largely by males; (2) the values taught in Mormon society (the world view she absorbed as a child) contrasted with those of the larger world; and (3) the challenge to be accepted among people not inclined to view Mormonism favorably.

---

18. "Home Affairs," *Woman's Exponent*, Sep. 15, 1878.

19. Shari Siebers Crall, "'Something More': A Biography of Martha Hughes Cannon," (honors thesis, Brigham Young University, 1985), 14; *Journal History of the Church*, Aug. 13, 1878, Church History Library, Church of Jesus Christ of Latter-day Saints, Salt Lake City. Some sources mistakenly state that Mattie was set apart by Taylor.

CHAPTER THREE

MEDICAL SCHOOL

Because many men were often absent serving missions for the church in the eastern states or in Europe, Brigham Young recognized the need for women to be more than homemakers. He is on record as saying, "We believe that women ... should ... study law or physics or become good bookkeepers and be able to do the business in any counting house." He also advised women to attend medical school: "The time has come for women to come forth as doctors in these valleys of the mountains." Consequently, the Relief Society supported a number of women who went east to obtain training.[1] Many of those earliest students attended the Women's Medical College in Philadelphia. Mattie charted a different course by attending co-educational medical schools in Ann Arbor, Michigan, and Philadelphia.

What was Mattie's life like after she struck out on her own, far from family and friends? Since her journals were destroyed,[2] there is no record to consult. However, she wrote voluminous letters to her husband, Angus M. Cannon, while in England in 1886–1887 to avoid arrest for being a plural wife. In one letter, dated November 1, 1886, she describes her time as a student:

> I would like to compare notes with you however during a period of four years of my life, that was my campaigning in the East of which

---

1. Vicky Burgess–Olson, ed., *Sister Saints* (Provo, UT: Brigham Young University Press, 1978), viii; Chris Rigby Arrington, "Pioneer Midwives," in Claudia L. Bushman, ed., *Mormon Sisters* (Cambridge, MA: Emmeline Press Ltd., 1976), 58.

2. Mattie kept journals her whole life and maintained extensive correspondence. However, her sense of privacy and fear of being judged (which intensified over the course of her life) led her to ask her son, James, to burn all her journals and papers upon her death. Sadly, he complied with her wishes.

I have told you nothing. "Exciting vicissitudes" does not express it. "Hair-breath escapes" more "appropos." ... The labyrinthine paths I trod during those four years of my girlish career—where sin was presented in almost every conceivable form—flattery, fascination, allurement, and sometimes threatening—each appearing on the "bill of fare" as related to human action. Nothing but a kind Providence could have given to me the "Will-o-the-wisp" sort of nature that I then exhibited, to see, to ponder, and then to be spirited away in time to avoid danger. ... Your speaking of "exciting vicissitudes," brought up a panorama before me, that would appear more appropriate to the realm of fiction, than to "chapters from *real life*."[3]

When Mattie matriculated at the University of Michigan on September 30, 1878, she entered a new world—one that was in the midst of change. The first female student graduated from the medical school in 1871—only seven years before Mattie arrived. The faculty had not been in favor of admitting women: "The medical co-education of the sexes is at best an experiment of doubtful utility, and one not calculated to increase the dignity of man, nor the modesty of women."[4] In an age with extreme ideas of propriety, the idea of having males and females together in classes that taught, among other things, human anatomy would be overwhelming.

The medical school faculty finally agreed to give women the entire course of study, but insisted on keeping the female students totally separate from the rest of the class,[5] by organizing an elaborate duplication of courses with an increase of $500 in professorial salaries.

By 1881, separate classes had practically ceased, but female medical students were still not allowed to sit in the same room with the male students. Possibly the women were given seats in the preparation room where they could hear the lectures but not be seen. However, practical anatomy—the most controversial class to be taught coeducationally—was taught separately until 1908.[6]

3. Constance L. Lieber and John Sillito, eds., *Letters from Exile: The Correspondence of Martha Hughes Cannon and Angus M. Cannon, 1886–1888* (Salt Lake City: Signature Books, 1989), 71.

4. Wilfred B. Shaw, ed., *The University of Michigan. An Encyclopedic Survey in Nine Parts* (Ann Arbor: University of Michigan Press, 1951), 4:859.

5. Shaw, *University of Michigan*, 1:26.

6. Shaw, *University of Michigan*, 2:794–95.

In general, the entering female students had a more thorough education than the male applicants: 85 percent of entering women had a bachelor's degree, but only 44 percent of entering men did. Applicants to the medical school had to demonstrate a knowledge of English and the art of composition, natural philosophy and natural sciences, elementary math (including algebra), and enough Latin or Greek to understand the technical language of medicine and to read and write prescriptions.[7] The school was transitioning from a two-year to a three-year curriculum, which was first put into effect for the 1880 entering class. Mattie graduated under the requirements for the two-year course.

Despite fundraisers on her behalf before she left Utah, Mattie had difficulty making ends meet. She helped defray her expenses by doing housework at the students' boarding house (where she washed dishes but refused to wash pans)[8] and by acting as coach and secretary to a wealthy student from Oregon named Bethenia Owens–Adair.[9]

The student register for the 1879–80 term lists Mattie as attending: "Seat #61; Hughes, Miss M. P.; Date of entrance: Sep. 30; Department R; Course 2; Term 2."[10] Listening to other students' recitations and preparing her own reawakened Mattie's goal of lecturing on public health matters and she spent some time roughing out plans for a lecture tour. Anxious to begin, she wrote to LDS Church president John Taylor on July 30, 1879, about her plans and asked his opinion. Her original letter is lost, but we have Taylor's August 11 answer: "Dear Sister, ... In our reflections on this matter, we think it would be better that you finish your studies before entering the lecture field; in the meantime, you can prepare your lecture and forward us a copy, and if deemed advisable that you proceed forthwith on your tour, we can telegraph you." Taylor further instructs her that if she does do a lecture tour, she must arrange for her father or a brother to accompany her, "for in traveling ... a suitable

---

7. Shaw, *University of Michigan*, 2:787.

8. Elizabeth C. McCrimmon to Claire Noall, Feb. 13, 1938, Special Collections, J. Willard Marriot Library, University of Utah, Salt Lake City.

9. McCrimmon to Noall, Feb. 13, 1938.

10. Karen M. Mason, Assistant Reference Archivist, Bentley Historical Library, University of Michigan to Constance L. Lieber, Apr. 18, 1988.

protection is essential." In the end, nothing came of this premature idea, but Mattie would more than fulfill that goal later in life.[11]

Mattie took courses in histology—using a microscope to study tissue samples—and apparently bought a microscope for personal use. She writes to Angus on June 18, 1887, recalling romance, inattention to studies, and their consequences: "I lost a microscope once through basking in the comforting society of a handsome southerner when I should have been studying my books … I do not regret [that] comforting process—it was interesting to be sure! Even if I did lose a microscope on the strength of it."[12]

Mattie was a serious and focused student: her class notebooks display no doodling or to-do lists scribbled in the margins, just notes and illustrations from the lectures. Clinical work for the medical students was woefully inadequate. It was possible for a medical student to graduate and go into practice without ever seeing a baby delivered.[13]

Candidates for an MD had to not only complete the necessary coursework, they also had to survive the ballot. Two Michigan physicians were appointed to serve as examiners together with the medical faculty and, by ballot, decide who would graduate. A full vote was fifty-six; a passing vote was thirty-five—about 62 percent. Besides surviving the ballot, graduates had to be twenty-one years old, demonstrate "good moral character," attend at least two full courses (of six to nine months each), and pass their exams. Mattie's class consisted of about 312 men and forty women; of those, seventy-seven men and fourteen women graduated.[14]

The *Woman's Exponent* reported Mattie's graduation: "We tender our sincere congratulations to Miss Mattie Paul Hughes who has recently passed her examination and will graduate in the Medical Class of '80 at the 30th Annual Commencement of the Department

---

11. John Taylor to "Sister" [Martha Hughes Cannon], July 30, 1879, John Taylor Papers, MS 1346, Church History Library, Church of Jesus Christ of Latter-day Saints, Salt Lake City.

12. Lieber and Sillito, *Letters from Exile*, 130.

13. Shaw, *University of Michigan*, 1:221, 1:226.

14. I have taken these numbers from *The Annual Announcement of the Department of Medicine and Surgery of the University of Michigan for 1880–1881* (Ann Arbor: University of Michigan Press, 1880).

of Medicine and Surgery of the University of Michigan; to be held in University Hall at 10 o'clock A.M. Thursday July 1st, 1880."[15]

Mattie herself wrote to the *Exponent* about her "day of days": "[W]ith two hundred and four other graduates I marched triumphantly onto the great platform, where we were presented with our diplomas amid the cheers of the crowded Hall and as we descended our floral gifts were handed us. Mine was a basket of beautiful flowers, rich and rare."[16] By then, her wardrobe was so shabby that she was overjoyed to receive presents from her sister, Mary, and her stepfather: a bonnet and a cloak, which she wore to her graduation.[17]

Mattie spent the summer after graduation in Algonac on the banks of the St. Clair River, practicing medicine and caring for the invalid wife of riverboat captain George Stomlar. His wife, Emily, was ailing and considered insane. Only twenty-seven years old, Emily was suffering from vesicovaginal fistula: an abnormal fistulous tract extending between the bladder and the vagina that allows a continuous involuntary discharge of urine into the vaginal vault. This was often caused by childbirth and could have a severe effect on the patient's emotional stability.[18] Mattie used a relatively new surgical procedure to cure Emily.

The *Marine City Reporter* praised Mattie for discovering the underlying cause of Stomlar's illness and performing the surgery that ultimately healed her. No copies of that issue of the *Reporter* exist, but the *Exponent* reprinted the text of the article: "A very successful surgical operation ... was performed in Algonac, on Wednesday, by Miss Mattie P. Hughes, M.D., with the assistance of Drs. Moore, of Algonac, and W. H. Smith, of St. Clair. Dr. Slocum had been invited to take part in the operation, but declined to play 'second fiddle' to a woman. ... [Neither of the others] felt that they were compromising their dignity by assisting a lady in a very difficult operation upon one of her own sex. Especially ... when the lady in question is such a genial and accomplished woman as Miss Hughes."

The article concludes with a final compliment for Mattie, but

---

15. "Home Affairs," *Woman's Exponent*, July 1, 1880, 20.
16. "Home Affairs," *Woman's Exponent*, July 15, 1880, 28.
17. Elizabeth C. McCrimmon to Claire Noall, Mar. 12, 1938.
18. See www.emedicine.medscape.com/article/267943-overview.

also with a not-so-subtle slur towards other women: "In the above case this young lady physician took the principal part in the work, and thus demonstrated by actual experience that some of her sex at least are capable of performing the most difficult and complicated operations in medical practice."[19]

In May 1881 Mattie entered the University of Pennsylvania. Women were first admitted to the university in the late 1870s, and in 1878 they were allowed to go into the Auxiliary School of Medicine, but only to selected lectures, and they could not be matriculated into the medical school itself. The Auxiliary School had been established in 1865 to address medical subjects that were not taught in the medical school, including comparative anatomy, botany, hygiene, medical jurisprudence, and toxicology.

It is likely that the course on hygiene was one of the things that attracted Mattie to the University of Pennsylvania. The course covered all the known conditions pertinent to individual and public health, including the causes of epidemics. The emphasis was on prevention.[20]

After Mattie attended the requisite lectures and wrote a thesis on mountain fever, the faculty of medicine and the trustees of the university recommended that she be awarded a BS on June 15, 1881, making her the first woman in the history of the university to receive a degree in course.[21] She graduated with a total of 43.75 points out of a possible 50.[22] Demonstrating that female students were still considered not quite on a par with their male counterparts, the four graduating men were awarded the degree of Doctor of Philosophy.

With the goal of preparing herself for public speaking, Mattie also enrolled as a student at the National School of Elocution and Oratory where she made a detailed study of the various styles of

19. "Editorial Notes," *Woman's Exponent*, Aug. 1, 1881.

20. The University of Pennsylvania granted the degree of Doctor of Philosophy to Mary Alice Bennett, MD, for her successful completion of the post-graduate course in medical science offered by the School of Auxiliary Medicine. Bennett, an 1876 graduate of the Women's Medical College of Pennsylvania, became the first woman to earn a degree at the University of Pennsylvania.

21. University of Pennsylvania, Minutes of Trustees, XI, June 6, 15, 1882, pp. 654, 663. See also "University Day Annual Commencement," *Philadelphia Inquirer*, June 16, 1882.

22. Minutes of Trustees; see also Saul Sack, *A History of Higher Education in Pennsylvania* (Harrisburg, PA: Pennsylvania Historical and Museum Commission, 1963), 2:563.

elocution and applied them to class readings.[23] The curriculum included vocal drills and a list of texts students used to practice evoking pathos, eloquence, tragedy, and humor.

We know Mattie made a careful study of the poem "Beautiful Snow" by Joseph Warren Watson because notice of her recitation of the poem appeared in the Philadelphia *Evening News*, reporting she gave the selection at an "entertainment" given by the National School on February 7, 1881, and did so with "scholarly ability."[24]

Upon her return to Utah, she joined the staff of the Deseret Hospital. The hospital had been established in Salt Lake City on July 15, 1882, with the intent that patients be aided (as Romania P. Penrose described it) by "physicians act[ing] upon the highest principles of skill and science, their works assisted by faith." Mattie was the resident physician. The Deseret Hospital had a "home-like feeling," and its patients were mostly "aged ladies" and young mothers. One visitor was impressed with Mattie: "She staggers not at the most difficult clinical or surgical work of the Hospital. She has at this time a case of the most intricate and complicated hip joint disease, which she is handling with remarked ability and satisfaction [especially considering her age] and brevity of practice."[25]

The general organization of a nineteenth-century hospital consisted of a consulting staff (older and well-established physicians who had no regular duties), a visiting or attending staff (active physicians who were in charge of patient care), a resident physician (or staff), and the junior physicians who carried out treatment details. The organization of the Deseret Hospital was similar. Dr. W. F. Anderson was the consulting physician and was available from 11:00 a.m. through 1:00 p.m. As resident physician, Mattie was always on call and lived in a room at the hospital. The hospital also had a dispensary and several nurses. Mattie was variously identified as the house surgeon (December 1882) and the house physician (January 1883). The *Deseret News* reported that "[her] intelligence and capacity is a subject of comment among those

23. Gilbert Austin, cited in Eugene Bahn and Margaret L. Bahn, *A History of Oral Interpretation* (Minneapolis: Burgess Publishing Co., 1970), 141.

24. "Home Affairs," *Woman's Exponent*, Mar. 1, 1881.

25. Mrs. B. Spurlock, "Salt Lake City Hospitals," *Woman's Exponent*, Nov. 1, 1884.

who have opportunities for observing her qualification." By November 1885 she had been appointed resident surgeon, replacing Ellen B. Ferguson, who had resigned.[26]

---

26. Ruth Abrams, *"Send Us a Lady Doctor": Women Doctors in America 1835–1920* (New York: W.W. Norton & Co., 1985), 163; *Deseret News*, Jan. 5, 1883; "Annual Meeting of the D.H.A." *Woman's Exponent*, June 1, 1883.

CHAPTER FOUR

MARRIAGE

Mattie was a focused but fun-loving young woman, in love with her religion and with the wider world: a woman who reveled in her strengths but also revealed her weaknesses. These attributes are amply demonstrated in her long correspondence with Barbara Replogle, a fellow student at the National School. The letters are frustratingly short and undetailed, as Barbara already knew Mattie's stories—but the letters show a different side of Mattie after she returned to Salt Lake City.

However, it is important to understand that these letters are, to a certain extent, staged documents. Mattie is creating a narrative that she hopes will be palatable to her friend's ear. That narrative changes and expands as Mattie begins to feel more comfortable with letting Barbara know certain details of her life in Utah—specifically her involvement with polygamy. It was at this time that Mattie began to develop the habit of keeping people at arm's length—a character trait that only intensified as she got older. Her letters are coupled with admonishments such as "do not mention that I enquired."[1]

On September 18, 1884, Mattie wrote Barbara, and although she had begun a courtship with fifty-year-old Angus M. Cannon, she did not give any hint of it. In fact, she discouraged any thought that she might be attached: "This is a busy career I have entered upon—yet I like it. But O how I long for some refining intellectual dessert to taper off with occasionally. If you were here, I should take time

---

1. Martha Maria Hughes Cannon to Barbara Replogle Atkinson, Oct. 2, 1884, MS 8867, Martha H. Cannon Collection, 1883–1912, Church History Library, Salt Lake City, also at catalog.lds.org, hereafter cited as Replogle Letters.

and practice Elocution with you with a vim, and discuss with you our heroes in literature; as well as the living masculine specimens we have come in contact with ... of course the time has not come in my case at least to make any definite progress in the masculine direction—Matrimony I refer to.[2]

Mattie was being disingenuous. Four days after writing that letter, she married Angus Munn Cannon. She was worried that Barbara might read newspaper accounts of Mattie being sought by federal marshals for unlawful cohabitation, so she tried to sidestep any idea of personal involvement as a plural wife, but she does tell Barbara that she is under bond to appear as the leading witness against one Samuel B. Smith, "who is being tried for polygamy."[3] "It is naturally supposed that the polygamous families engage me [to deliver their children]. Hence, I am considered an important witness, and if it can be proven that these children have actually come into the world, their fathers will be sent to jail for five (5) years. By this time, Barb, you will think me a reprobate, having so much to do with the courts—but this is the outcome of me being a Mormon and living in a Mormon community."[4]

Mattie had a strong personality, but Elizabeth Rachel reports, "In my father, I believe, she met a more masterful character."[5] Rachel says that her father was "handsome, magnetic, with the gift of language. [His] chief characteristic was his spirituality. Strongly spiritual herself, this appealed to [Mattie]."[6] But she possibly discounted what this devotion to duty would mean to a marriage where his time was already divided among three other wives.

Mattie met Angus Munn Cannon at the Deseret Hospital in Salt Lake City, where he was a member of the board of directors. The account of their first meeting is perhaps apocryphal, but it is

2. Replogle Letters, Sep. 18, 1884.

3. Samuel H. B. Smith was arrested on the charge of unlawful cohabitation on April 23, 1885, and found guilty on February 9, 1886. There is no record of Mattie appearing at his trial as a witness. See Abraham H. Cannon, Diary, Apr. 23, 1885 and Feb. 9, 1886, MS 1929, Church History Library, Church of Jesus Christ of Latter-day Saints, Salt Lake City.

4. Replogle Letters, May 1, 1885.

5. Elizabeth Cannon McCrimmon to Clair Noall, Feb. 13, 1938, Special Collections, J. Willard Marriott Library, University of Utah, Salt Lake City.

6. Elizabeth Cannon McCrimmon, "Dr. Martha Hughes Cannon, First Woman State Senator in America," Seydell Quarterly 11, no. 2 (Winter 1959): 6–8.

certainly entertaining: Mattie was on her hands and knees cleaning a hospital floor, and Angus was blocking her path. Rather than give him the respect due his position as president of the Salt Lake Stake, she ordered, "Stand aside!" Although onlookers were shocked, Angus was intrigued.[7]

Angus did not dare record anything about their courtship, even in his private journals. Mattie may have—but since her journals were destroyed, we will never know. One hint is found in the journal of Abraham H. Cannon. He writes on Friday, January 30, 1885: "Uncle Angus ... [was] at my house in the evening for a short time ... having made an appointment with Dr. Mattie Hughes." Perhaps it was to get her medical opinion on something; more probably it was an assignation.[8]

Their friendship deepened through Angus's continuing visits to the Deseret Hospital; they certainly also met from time to time in a medical capacity, as Mattie attended to Angus's other wives and his children. All private meetings would have been cloaked in secrecy. The necessary stealth surrounding what passed for dates, and the danger Angus put himself in when meeting her, may have added to the excitement of their courtship. Were they successful in keeping things secret? Certainly not. As becomes evident in Angus's subsequent trial for cohabitation, many people suspected, and a few may have even known. But no one was talking.

Even when Mattie and Angus were married—on October 6, 1884, in the Endowment House in Salt Lake City—the wedding was conducted in such secrecy that Mattie's own mother was ignorant of the ceremony.[9]

The fallout from Angus and Mattie's marriage was swift. One wonders at Angus's impetuousness, as he certainly knew what contracting an illegal polygamous marriage in 1884 would mean. The potential danger may not have been as evident to Mattie. The fact is that Angus was smitten with Mattie and that she adored him.[10]

---

7. McCrimmon to Noall, Feb. 13, 1938.

8. Abraham H. Cannon, Diary, Jan. 30, 1885.

9. Constance L. Lieber and John Sillito, eds., *Letters from Exile: The Correspondence of Martha Hughes Cannon and Angus M. Cannon, 1886–1888* (Salt Lake City: Signature Books, 1989), 71.

10. Lieber and Sillito, *Letters from Exile*, 224.

The *Salt Lake Herald* reported on January 20, 1885, that "the air was full of arrests and rumors of arrests." One of those arrested was Angus M. Cannon. He was charged with lascivious cohabitation and polygamy under the terms of the Edmunds Act, his bond placed at $2,500. Two of his wives, Amanda and Clara, and several of his children were subpoenaed as witnesses.[11]

The preliminary hearing began at 2:00 p.m. on Wednesday, January 21, 1885, before Commissioner William McKay.[12] According to Abraham Cannon, Angus was confident he would be cleared.[13] However, not all the subpoenaed witnesses showed up. Chief among the missing witnesses was Mattie.[14] She was determined not to appear in court, believing, in contrast to her husband, that Angus stood little likelihood of being acquitted.

Angus M. Cannon Jr., one of the first witnesses, was brought in by a policeman, as he was already in custody for public drunkenness. His testimony concerning Mattie was confusing at best. It is difficult to know if the confusion resulted from deliberate obfuscation or from his inebriation: "I may have stated father was married, will state on oath I never did say so, but I may have said so, but I say I know I never said so, I may have lied. I did lie when I said I may have said so. Just had the idea it may be so."

And then the main point of his rambling testimony: "I thought they were getting a little too intimate; she is young and fascinating you know, and I was afraid that she might have caught my father's eye and I was a little jealous on my mother's account."

How difficult for a son, loyal to his mother, to find his father attracted, perhaps even married, to a woman the son also found alluring—and, because of polygamy, might also have courted and wed.

On Saturday morning, January 24, the Cannon polygamy case was called in McKay's court and the district attorney had to announce that

---

11. "Local Briefs," *Salt Lake Herald,* Jan. 21, 1885.

12. A commissioner was a quasi-official person hired by the court to help the judge's case load. The chief justice at the time was Charles S. Zane. W. H. Dickson was a prosecuting attorney who often argued his case in Commissioner McKay's court. Frank H. Dyer was the US marshal who figured most often in the Cannon cases.

13. "Local Briefs," *Salt Lake Herald,* Jan. 21, 1885.

14. The trial was reported extensively in all three Salt Lake City newspapers: *Salt Lake Tribune, Deseret News,* and *Salt Lake Herald,* beginning with the Jan. 21, 1885, issues.

his officers had still been unable to find Mattie Hughes. McKay concluded that the evidence on the charge of polygamy was incomplete, but that Angus would be held on the count of unlawful cohabitation. Members of Angus's family were secretly laughing at the hapless officers. Abraham Cannon recorded on January 22: "Uncle Angus' case was continued today without any new developments. The principal witness, Miss Hughes, had not yet been found by the marshals although she has been on the street attending to her patients."[15]

January 27 found the defendant, the witnesses, the lawyers, and federal officials once more gathered in McKay's office. "But the long-looked-for witness, Miss Mattie Hughes, was not there. The keen-sighted Deputy Marshals had failed to find her." The *Deseret News* wrote "the leading question on the street today is 'Where is Miss Mattie Hughes?'"[16]

One enterprising federal marshal finally caught up with Mattie at the Deseret Hospital and served her with a subpoena to appear the next Monday before the grand jury where (according to the *Deseret News*) she would be required to tell what she knew concerning the Cannon case and (according to the *Salt Lake Tribune*) what she "don't remember" about her marriage to Cannon. Mattie acknowledged to the officer that she had been dodging them or, in her words, "giving the boys a lark."[17]

Mattie continued to attend to her duties as house physician at the Deseret Hospital, the *Deseret News* reporting on January 28 that she had assisted in a lithotomy (removal of a bladder, kidney, or urinary tract stone) on a four-year-old boy. Angus attended to his church duties as stake president as best he could. Abraham recorded that he, "Called at Uncle Angus' to see if I could do anything, but found all serene."[18]

Mattie must have begun to wonder what her own situation would be if Angus were sent to prison, as she was by now expecting her first child.

Angus was arrested once more on January 27 and was indicted for lascivious cohabitation on February 7, his bonds further fixed at

15. Abraham H. Cannon, Diary, Oct. 1879–Jun. 1881.

16. "Where Is that Witness?" *Deseret News,* Jan. 27, 1885.

17. "Mattie P. Caught," *Salt Lake Tribune,* and "Dr. Mattie Hughes Subpoenaed," *Deseret News Semi-Weekly,* Jan. 27, 1885.

18. Abraham H. Cannon, Diary, Jan. 20, 1885.

$2,000. The warrant for his arrest charged that Angus, prior to January 1, 1884, married Amanda Mousley, his lawful wife, in Salt Lake City. He was also accused of marrying Mattie Hughes on June 1, 1884, while un-divorced from Amanda, thus committing the crime of polygamy. Furthermore, he was charged with living with more than one woman for over ten years, namely Amanda Mousley Cannon, Sarah Mousley, Clara C. Valentine Mason, and Mattie Hughes.[19]

Throughout the whole procedure, neither prosecution nor defense considered the question of whether or not Angus was guilty: both camps knew that he was. What remained was posturing within the law to see if they could get him off or, alternately, convicted.

In April the two sides were still wrangling over the question of how unlawful cohabitation should be interpreted or proven. The question before the court on April 19 was "whether in a case of unlawful cohabitation it was necessary to prove sexual intercourse, or is living in the same house with two or more women whom a man acknowledges as his wives sufficient." Any hope the defense held out was dashed when Judge Charles Shuster Zane ruled "that the latter was sufficient. This virtually decided the case and … the jury brought in a verdict of guilty."[20] Angus was delivered to prison on May 9, 1885.

By entering into a polygamous marriage relationship, Mattie embraced a principle that would bring her joy and that she never denounced, but that also complicated her life. From now on, whatever she did, professionally and privately, was seen through that lens.

19. "Further Particulars of the Arrest of President Angus M. Cannon," *Deseret News Semi-Weekly*, Jan. 28, 1885. The newspaper got the order of wives wrong. Angus had married Amanda and her older sister, Sarah, on the same day at the behest of President Young. Because Amanda was Angus's first love, he never revealed until much later which one he had married first, so Amanda acted as the "first wife" and was his hostess. Amanda was not, as the paper reported, his "lawful wife"—he had married Sarah first. Madelyn Stewart Silver Palmer, "Undaunted and Courageous to the End. Sarah Maria Mousley Cannon (1828–1912)," 5–6, 11, copy in my possession.

20. Abraham H. Cannon, Journal, Apr. 29, 1885.

CHAPTER FIVE

EXILE

When Angus was released from prison in December 1885, Mattie was caring for their infant daughter, Elizabeth Rachel, born September 13, 1885, in Grantsville, Utah. If either he or Mattie had any hope that their relationship would normalize, they were both disappointed. The zeal of the federal marshals to convict polygamists gave neither of them any rest.

Church leaders, including Angus, had gone "underground"—a complicated system of safe houses and watchers that helped them avoid arrest. Instead of going into hiding, Mattie decided to go to England. Angus wrote in his journal on March 23, 1886: "I am told friend wants to go to England and I consent … I leave here tonight with the saddest heart I ever felt."[1]

Mattie landed in Liverpool on May 1st and spent her first few days at the church offices in Liverpool where she met Emily Wells Grant, another plural wife in exile. Emily was amused and amazed to see Mattie, though she thought Mattie was very wise to have left Utah, writing to her husband and future church president, Heber J. Grant, that if anyone were to catch a glimpse of "little Miss Munn," they would be able to convict the whole family.[2]

After leaving the Liverpool office, Mattie went to Birmingham where she spent approximately two unhappy weeks with her uncle

---

1. Angus M. Cannon, Journals, Mar. 23, 1886, Angus M. Cannon Collection, 1854–1920, MS 1200, Church History Library, Salt Lake City.
2. Emily Wells Grant to Heber J. Grant, May 17, 1886, Heber J. Grant Papers, Church History Library, Salt Lake City. Emily was the daughter of England Mission president Daniel H. Wells. She used the name "Mary" or "Mary Ann Harris" and referred to her husband as "Eli Harris" to avoid discovery.

Thomas Evans and then escaped to the country. She explained to Angus: "[His wife] had a cataleptic fit, and one of her little girls fell down stairs and injured her head. ... Uncle is inclined to investigate the Gospel and Satan is making himself manifest in various ways."[3] Mattie's next destination was the residence of Joseph Twyman, a distant relative who lived in the village of Wolverton, about six miles from Stratford-upon-Avon.[4]

Mattie stayed in the area throughout the summer, finding two different lodgings in nearby Norton Lindsey. She did not have fond memories of the first place, writing to Angus: "Positively you would not believe me should I attempt to describe it ... a row of tumble-down ruins [built about 1550], one end of it inhabited by the family I am living with."[5] Her next boarding place was worse. She found the couple she lodged with, Mr. and Mrs. Mark Coldrey, repulsive. She wrote to Angus in early June: "I have since learned that [Mr. Coldrey] has been laid up with [syphilis] three times and joined the Indian army because he had two girls in the 'family way.' That accounts for the bad smell. ... He is a regular rogue and only about thirty 3 or 4 now. ... Most horrible of all, he insisted on frequently kissing little Elizabeth."[6] Fed up with the Coldreys, Mattie searched for other lodgings. By midsummer, she had been joined by another plural wife, Anna Ballmer, whom Mattie always referred to as "Mrs. Hull." They lodged in the two halves of Ivy Close Cottage with "poor, honest sort of folk."[7]

Wolverton was ideally placed for the American tourist: Leamington Spa, Warwick Castle, the ruins of Kenilworth Castle, and Stratford-upon-Avon were all within either walking distance or a short carriage ride, and Mattie visited them all.

---

3. Constance L. Lieber and John Sillito, eds., *Letters from Exile: The Correspondence of Martha Hughes Cannon and Angus M. Cannon, 1886–1888* (Salt Lake City: Signature Books, 1989), 13.

4. Wolverton is still a small village. The 2011 population was 212.

5. Lieber and Sillito, *Letters from Exile*, 100.

6. Lieber and Sillito, *Letters from Exile*, 27.

7. Lieber and Sillito, *Letters from Exile*, 54; Ken F. Chapman to Constance L. Lieber, June 29, 1990. Anna Margarete Ballmer Schettler married her second husband, Fredrick August Engelbert Meyer, on May 8, 1885. Mattie knew Anna before either was in exile. In May 1884, Mattie moved her medical offices to the home of Paul A. Schettler, who was Ballmer's first husband. He died on November 3, 1884. "Those Who Are Coming and Going," *Salt Lake Herald*, May 30, 1884.

While visiting the Shakespeare Museum, she indulged in a fa-
vorite tourist pastime: sitting in Shakespeare's chair. "Just then
Elizabeth, in unmistakable signs declared that she wanted a 'ikkle
dop of titty' [a little drop of titty], so I gave her some to the amusement of a party of six from Aston ... and one of the ladies remarked
that the child would in all probability develop Shakespearean in-
stincts after going through so remarkable a process."[8]

Gradually, the villagers became aware that Mattie and Mrs. Hull
were not quite who they claimed to be. Rumors began flying about,
necessitating their departure. "But why leave our rural retreat you
ask?" Mattie wrote to Angus

> For various reasons, chief among them this, that we remained such a
> mystery that the villagers were becoming exercised about it. And so the
> buzz increased, until we were discussed in the highways, byways, private
> gatherings, at firesides, and particularly at the "Red Horse" and "Bell Inn"
> over the beer pots.[9] ... Latterly the name Mormon became associated
> with us and the tune changed. Those who did not know the meaning
> of the word, and they a vast majority, were enlightened by those who
> thought they did. A result of which as I was wheeling little Elizabeth
> past a threshing machine one day, one of the [farm laborers] remarked,
> 'get thee up and help we the work, and get thee petticoats full o' dust and
> then let one o' we men to dust them out, as thou hast no man.[10]

After she left Wolverton, Mattie's exile took on a peripatetic nature
and she did not remain very long in any one place. Between January
and mid-September 1887, she lived in London and Brighton, interspersed with shorter stays in Liverpool and a five-day trip to Wales.
Her letters to Angus changed in tone. She was less upbeat, less enthusiastic about life abroad. Now everything just seemed hard. Elizabeth
was not well, and Mattie was anxious about matters at home.

In her letters Mattie was often complacent about her life in
England though sometimes excited about the new sights and adventures. But as time went on, she struggled more and more often with
jealousy, trying to keep her faith that entering into a polygamous

---

8. Lieber and Sillito, *Letters from Exile*, 25.
9. The Bell Inn is in Snitterfield; it is now called the Fox Hunter. The Red Horse
Inn, which was between Norton Lindsey and Wolverton, has been demolished.
10. Lieber and Sillito, *Letters from Exile*, 85–86.

marriage had been the right course to take. During the rather fleeting times when she regretted her marriage and became bitter, she took her frustrations out on Angus. In one letter, she worries that she will have to appear before the grand jury when she returns to Utah: "On which occasion I will swear by all that is staple, that I have *not*, in any *manner, shape or conceivable form whatever*, been 'held out,' 'associated with,' looked upon as such—or experienced the delight thereof, imagined the condition—or even dreamed it, or any other infernal twist they like to connect with the term 'wife.'"[11]

Those who entered into plural marriages early, such as Angus's first three wives, initially had the opportunity to live in peace as family units—what Mattie referred to as an "ordinary plurality." That was in stark contrast with her own situation and that of others who entered the system during the 1880s when persecutions were at their most intense. In a letter to Angus written from England, she expressed a desire that she and others in her situation might someday "publicly associate with, accompany & share the honors of our noble lord. I think we would get along nicely with an *ordinary* plurality, but we are having such an *extraordinary* one now that I get a bit discouraged at times and wonder if some of us ever will have any respectable married life."[12] Angus wrote to her that they "should yet have many, many happy days in each other's society."[13] She countered that she feared she would have to "look forward to the next stage of existence for the fulfillment of [those] hopes."[14]

Mattie was also jealous of the other wives, especially Maria Bennion, whom Angus married while Mattie was preparing to go to England, and would often vent her feelings in her letters, writing to Angus: "I think you got the idea I was jealous. ... I trust, dear, that if I am so disgustingly mean or foolish as to get jealous over the discharge of your duty to others, and obligations and attentions which is their *absolute* right to receive from you, I will have sufficient strength and grace from God to thoroughly eradicate the same, and replace

---

11. Lieber and Sillito, *Letters from Exile*, 56.

12. Lieber and Sillito, *Letters from Exile*, 121.

13. Lieber and Sillito, *Letters from Exile*, 36. Here Mattie quotes from Angus's letter, which is not extant.

14. Lieber and Sillito, *Letters from Exile*, 121.

it with a less selfish feeling."[15] She even resorts to humor to excuse her jealous comments to her husband: "*Why* blame we women when you men are such *magnets* that draw us to you in spite of ourselves."[16]

Mattie could never really resolve her fear that Angus loved her less—or perhaps not at all—and continued to waver between attempting to find peace with her situation and giving full voice to her frustrations and fears.

Additionally, she was depressed. "I have 'stuck it out' so far, with the result of wearing myself out—so that I have no ambition left. ... I am growing indifferent to everything that once gave keenest pleasure ... my poor precious baby feels the depression that is upon me, and for her dear sake I must rouse me from this lethargy—were it not for her and the religion of our God I should never want to see Salt Lake again but seek some other spot and strive to forget what a failure my life has been."[17]

That despair culminated in a letter she wrote to Angus shortly before she left England for the United States. Elizabeth was sick and ill-behaved, and Mattie had reached the end of her emotional resources. This letter was the only one Angus destroyed, but in his reply to her, he quoted from it:

Had you said you were 'pleased and pained;' pleased to have heard of my accident and pained that I was not killed outright, instead of saying 'pleased and thankful that you were preserved,' I should have better understood you when I read what you said further on in your letter regarding the deception I have practiced upon you, i.e., pretending to love you while my heart was estranged and my feelings flowed in other directions. [It is impossible for me] *in my maudlin way* to convince you, that although I do say it in all truthfulness before my God, though you have gone through trials you believe to be cruel with fire and brimstone, you have not done so without my warmest love. You may doubt it with your whole soul, but you are loved by the man you have gone through everything for and sacrificed everything on earth.[18]

Mattie's response was quick and full of emotion: "Oh Papa, Papa!!

15. Lieber and Sillito, *Letters from Exile*, 179.
16. Lieber and Sillito, *Letters from Exile*, 74.
17. Lieber and Sillito, *Letters from Exile*, 212.
18. Lieber and Sillito, *Letters from Exile*, 224–25.

I feel like crying myself sick to think what a wicked girl I have been to hurt your feelings as I have: I did not know what mean things I had written until I read your quotations from my letter. I was half beside myself when I wrote, sobbing & hysterical. ... The only thing I can do now is to humbly ask forgiveness. ... I do not expect the wound to be entirely healed until I see you, when I feel sanguine that I can prove to you how sincerely I repent of my evil words."[19]

On December 3, 1887, Mattie and Elizabeth boarded the *Arizona* in Liverpool and enjoyed a luxurious stateroom, which Mattie described as "large, airy ... and everything comfortable. ... I am fixed fine." She had hoped a letter would be waiting for her when they docked in Canada around December 13, 1887, but what she received was much better: Angus was there to meet them.

Elizabeth wrote that when Angus met the ship, "the three of us crossed on the international bridge into the United States. Father then got nervous [fearing federal marshals would discover and arrest him] and rushed back into Canada ... [and then] back into the U.S. 'What are you doing?' asked mother. 'I'm thinking!' replied he. 'Wouldn't it be cheaper to think in one place?' suggested mother." It cost $2.50 every time they crossed the bridge.[20]

Rather than return immediately to Salt Lake City, Mattie chose to go to Algonac and check up on her former patient Emily Stomlar. Mattie and Elizabeth were there by December 16, 1887. After a three-year stay in an England, which Mattie termed primitive by Salt Lake City standards, arriving in Algonac must have seemed like an even further step back in time. A small waterfront settlement on the St. Clair River, Algonac had no automobiles, no electricity, no city water, no railroad, and a population barely approaching 1,000. The inhabitants lit their homes with kerosene lamps. Travel—if not by boat—was mostly on horseback. It was not easy for Mattie and Elizabeth to get there from Detroit, which was only about fifty miles southeast of Algonac. They left Detroit by train, changed in Lennox, and then boarded a one-carriage train to St. Clair. From there they could either travel

19. Lieber and Sillito, *Letters from Exile*, 238.
20. Elizabeth Cannon Porter McCrimmon, "Reminiscences of Angus Munn Cannon by his Daughter Elizabeth Cannon Porter McCrimmon," undated manuscript in my possession.

sixteen miles "in an open conveyance" or take a ferry boat. The winter temperature was frigid; Mattie chose to go by ferry.

She was unimpressed with Algonac and the St. Clair: "This is such a dreary little country place with the great frozen river stretching far in front of us—with its unkempt waste of Indian Reservation beyond." She had only experienced the area "in its summer loveliness, [the river's] surface roseate with morning sunbeams of its crystal waters reflecting the different hued lights from the many crafts that dotted its surface at evening."[21] Mattie remained with the Stomlars until the end of February. By then, Elizabeth had contracted chicken pox, and other children in the house had scarlet fever, so Mattie sought other lodgings. When Elizabeth also came down with scarlet fever, the woman with whom Mattie boarded wanted her to leave lest her own children get sick. Mattie paid her extra, promising to isolate herself and Elizabeth. Mattie retained enough of a sense of humor to write to Angus dryly: "This is measles, chicken pox, and scarlatina she has had since I have been from home. Whooping Cough would about complete the catalogue of infantile disorders, but I am not at all ambitious for her to take it."[22]

Elizabeth remained ill for long enough that Mattie decided the time was right to seek medical care in Ann Arbor. But the St. Claire River was blocked by ice, delaying their departure. Finally, on April 26 she wrote to Angus that she had arrived in Ann Arbor and was able to rent the room she stayed in as a student. "I am now domiciled in my little upstairs back room, where I spent one year and a half of my college days—and dreary and 'pokey' [small, shabby] enough it seems."[23]

Mattie had returned to Ann Arbor for the express purpose of taking Elizabeth to her old professor Dr. Edward S. Dunster to be examined for kidney problems or bladder stones. Mattie also wanted to seek treatment for her womb troubles and so anticipated remaining in Ann Arbor for three months. However, it was not to be. She wrote to Angus: "You see, we are here at last, only to find Prof. Dunster dying—the one man above all others whom I would trust with the examination of my precious Little One."[24]

---

21. Lieber and Sillito, *Letters from Exile*, 247, 254, 259.
22. Lieber and Sillito, *Letters from Exile*, 266.
23. Lieber and Sillito, *Letters from Exile*, 275.
24. Lieber and Sillito, *Letters from Exile*, 276.

Elizabeth was examined by a Dr. Vaughn instead, who wanted to "put her under chloroform & sound the bladder." But she had been so ill for so long, he worried she might not withstand that treatment and instead prescribed "tonics, beef tea & new milk to build her body up." To Mattie's distress, Elizabeth would not cooperate. "She is a miserable eater. 'Peanuts' are the only thing she cares to eat at all and they are *fearful* things to digest, so I let her yell rather than buy them for her."[25] Vaughn's eventual diagnosis was a relief: Elizabeth had a severe inflammation at the neck of the bladder, which could be cured without surgery. Mattie sought no treatment for herself; instead, she attended Dunster's funeral.[26]

Mattie's last exile letter to Angus was written from Chicago on May 11, 1888: "I have lived a *life* in the past three years, as compared with which the preceding twenty-eight years seemed but as child's play. But I have no regrets. I am willing and not afraid to tread the paths of my destiny whether they be rugged or whether they be smooth. God is just and merciful, and although He has at times permitted me to feel the *thorns* of life, He has also provided beautiful Oases, in which to bask and feel 'what a glorious thing to live.'"[27]

When Mattie reached Salt Lake City, she was not in good health, either physically or emotionally. She feared that Angus would think she was a "chronic grunter," she complained so often about her health. Mattie had sought medical help in England twice. On one occasion she consulted a Dr. Croft, but was not impressed. "He charged me a good price but did me no good. I soon saw he did not understand the case and dismissed him. He did not know I was an M.D."[28] She also sought help at St. Thomas' Hospital in London, but when she discovered she would not be examined by a physician but must "submit to the manipulations of students," she declined treatment.[29]

---

25. Lieber and Sillito, *Letters from Exile,* 278.

26. Lieber and Sillito, *Letters from Exile,* 278.

27. Lieber and Sillito, *Letters from Exile,* 277.

28. Lieber and Sillito, *Letters from Exile,* 155. Rev. Nightengale told me an old lady in his district thought there may have been a Dr. Croft in Snitterfield (letter to Lieber, May 9, 1989). This was confirmed by Christine Woodland, assistant archivist at the Warwickshire County Council Record Office, in a letter to me dated May 23, 1989, that Thomas Hardman Wilson Croft did live and practice medicine in Snitterfield during that period.

29. Lieber and Sillito, *Letters from Exile,* 170.

From her descriptions of what she called "womb trouble," it would seem she was suffering from a prolapsed uterus. She complained incessantly about a sensation of heaviness, or pulling, in her pelvis, as well as extreme discomfort when lifting or carrying Elizabeth, or even just when walking—all common symptoms.

Another constant theme—almost bordering on obsession—was that her health was affected adversely by Salt Lake City's high altitude. Her conviction that living at the "level of the sea" would solve most of her medical difficulties became more pronounced while she was in England. She wrote to Angus just a few months after her arrival: "Oh! I begin to feel like I used to when I was a rollicking college girl. Health is everything in this life—jostling with the world is fun when one has good health to back them. If my head gets bad when I reach the high altitude of Utah again, I shall say good-bye to that section, as dearly as I love it, and make a permanent home near the level of the sea."[30]

Being at sea level may have been a factor in Mattie's improved health, but a more likely reason was her leaving the physical and mental stress of her polygamous marriage and medical practice behind.

But plenty of stress came from Elizabeth, a sickly child who was indulged by her mother and became spoiled, ill-tempered, and prone to tantrums. Mattie's aunt in Birmingham (ill-tempered herself) pegged Elizabeth immediately, telling Mattie, "The little pale-faced madame has been thoroughly spoiled, and you will have enough to put up with before you get through with her."[31] Indeed, Mattie had to put up with "enough" and more. She described a scene at the dinner table at the church mission office in Liverpool shortly before she left to return to the United States: "At table babe acted most *outrageous*, disgusting everybody with her tantrums, eating nothing herself, not letting me have any peace pulling, hauling and screaming at me. ... I have humored her to death until all conclude she is a thoroughly ruined child."[32]

Mattie spoiled Elizabeth and tolerated such extreme behavior because she was afraid Elizabeth would die. "I want you to pray

---

30. Lieber and Sillito, *Letters from Exile*, 19.
31. Lieber and Sillito, *Letters from Exile*, 12.
32. Lieber and Sillito, *Letters from Exile*, 232.

mightily," she begged Angus, "that she may *live*." Mattie was aware what certain symptoms could mean but did not seem to be able to detach herself emotionally sufficiently to make a calm assessment of Elizabeth's case. Mattie recognized that she could not regard her daughter's condition subjectively: "I cannot think she will be taken from me and yet her condition makes me extremely nervous. 'A little knowledge is a dangerous thing.' If I was in total ignorance of certain symptoms, I should not worry so."[33]

Now returned home, Mattie knew what she wanted: to practice medicine again, to visit family and friends with whom she had lost contact, and to have some sort of family life with Angus and her daughter.

---

33. Lieber and Sillito, *Letters from Exile*, 144.

CHAPTER SIX

PICKING UP THE PIECES

After her long exile abroad, Mattie tried to reorganize her life, both professionally and personally, as she and Elizabeth stayed with her mother and stepfather.[1] Mattie soon discovered that she had returned to a Utah that was little changed from the one she had left. Polygamists (her husband included) were still in hiding, and federal marshals were still interested in convicting Angus via Mattie. Mattie suspected this would be the case even prior to her return, writing to Angus: "To return home with a darling baby, and yet be an unacknowledged wife, is going to be harder to bear than the loneliness of exile life."[2]

Her glum expectations were realized immediately upon her return to Salt Lake City. Angus was also there, but she saw so little of him that Elizabeth could be forgiven for not realizing that all three were living in the same city. Within days, Mattie wrote to him: "'So near and yet so far.' The separation seems almost as great as when a continent stretched between us. ... This morning our little treasure said, 'Come Mamma, let us go to 'Ootah' to see my papa.' It touched me, steeled as I am against emotional exhibitions. To think the child has reached her age and knows nothing of her father."[3]

Their relationship had changed since the days of their courtship.

---

1. Letters to Barbara Replogle Atkinson, Martha H. Cannon collection, 1883–1912, MS 8867, Aug. 10, 1888, Church History Library, Church of Jesus Christ of Latter-day Saints, Salt Lake City. Hereafter Replogle Letters.

2. Constance L. Lieber and John Sillito, eds., *Letters from Exile: The Correspondence of Martha Hughes Cannon and Angus M. Cannon, 1886–1888* (Salt Lake City: Signature Books, 1989), 184.

3. Lieber and Sillito, *Letters from Exile*, 281–82.

Mattie was emotional and needy while the more reserved Angus was busy with his church duties and other families.

Perhaps Angus had expected that Mattie would still resemble the young wife, head-over-heels in love, who had gone into exile to protect him. If so, he was disappointed. As he wrote to her, "Were you less self-reliant and resolute, I think I should feel more at home in your company. As it is, I would like to know that I possess some qualities that a woman of your recognized ability could discern as being that which should adorn the character of a man. If I knew that I was possessed of those qualities that you could esteem and make you happy, I should be one of the most happy men living."[4]

Eventually, Mattie moved her medical practice to John W. Young's office in downtown Salt Lake City, which was, as Elizabeth later wrote, large and lucrative.[5] Mattie was very busy but had no office or home of her own yet. That may have been acceptable when Mattie was just out of school, but now she expected something more and nagged Angus to provide it. By the beginning of November 1888, she reported to Barbara Replogle that she had "rented an office near Main Street and have a nice housekeeper and we keep house on a small scale, my little girl is with me, and she is such a Jewel—I am building a neat little structure that will answer the purpose of office and residence when completed, but it will not be hardly fit to move into until Spring."[6]

Angus's finances were no better than they had ever been, and it is almost certain that Mattie paid for much of this house herself. Elizabeth recalls the house as having one-and-a-half stories. "Downstairs there was [a] parlor, dining room, hall, office, bathroom and kitchen. The middle rooms were large—18 x 23 [feet], which was useful as we had to sleep in them. The upstairs, where the bedrooms were to be, was never finished. [It] was just a big attic. I usually slept in the hall with the hired girl."[7]

At thirty-one, Mattie found that she did not have the stamina

---

4. Lieber and Sillito, *Letters from Exile*, 209.

5. Mary Idelia Porter Ober Nichols, "History of Elizabeth Rachel Cannon Porter Mc-Crimmon Compiled by Her Daughter," Jan. 1989, 6, copy in the possession of Blaine Brady.

6. Replogle Letters, Nov. 10, 1888.

7. Elizabeth Cannon McCrimmon, untitled, undated partial manuscript. Copy in my possession.

she'd taken for granted as a newly minted physician. "I am getting on slowly but surely with my practice and am busy as is consistent with health at the present time," she wrote to Barbara Replogle.[8] In addition to attending to her patients, Mattie had committed to give weekly lectures on personal hygiene to the young ladies attending the Salt Lake Stake Academy, a private school under LDS Church administration, where both religious and secular subjects were taught. Mattie had been appointed "Lady Superintendent." She did not care for this assignment, complaining to Barbara that "there is so much mock modesty with young ladies of their age—Still, I suppose it is my duty to remove it as much as possible."[9]

By 1889 Mattie had opened a nursing school, modeled on the Boston training school for nurses. The objective of the school was focused on bettering the situation of women, "to make educated nurses of women and girls, and prepare them for competent work either in hospital or private practice." Her advertisement in the *Woman's Exponent* assured future students that she had "the needful apparatus, etc., the best charts, books and [a] skeleton." Tuition per term was $25.00. The first term was completed on May 4. She taught "all the branches of nursing," drilled her students on calisthenics, and taught Swedish massage, although Mattie did not perform massage herself, because, as Elizabeth wrote, Mattie was such a small woman "it taxed her strength too much." She also offered courses on obstetrics.[10]

The *Woman's Exponent* was enthusiastic about the school's opening, writing, "All who are acquainted with Dr. Hughes will feel as we do, that she is competent by education and training to give the necessary instruction, and has the high moral courage and independence necessary for the work she is about to undertake."[11]

By 1890 her practice was doing well enough that she decided to

---

8. Replogle Letters, Nov. 10, 1888.

9. Replogle Letters, Nov. 10, 1888. The Salt Lake Stake Academy had been founded in 1887 and was supervised by Angus, who was chair of the State Board of Education. In 1889 its name was changed to "Latter-day Saints College."

10. "A Training School for Nurses," *Woman's Exponent*, Jan. 1, 1889, 117; advertisement, *Woman's Exponent*, Jan. 15, 1889, 128; and advertisement, *Woman's Exponent*, May 1, 1889, 184.

11. "A Training School for Nurses," *Woman's Exponent*, Jan. 1, 1889, 117.

take a break from business[12]—or so she told Barbara. In actuality, she was going into exile once more. On May 19, 1890, Mattie delivered her second child, James Hughes Cannon, in the home of John Henry Smith. Dr. Ellis Shipp delivered the baby. Angus wrote in his journal that Shipp was "obliged to use instruments to save [the] life of mother and child." When he finally saw his wife, she "was delirious from drugs."[13] They decided to name the baby James Hughes after Mattie's stepfather and father. He weighed 11.75 pounds, which, Angus proudly recorded, was "the largest boy born to [him]."[14] To celebrate, Angus visited Elizabeth, who was staying with Mattie's parents, and presented her with a nickel.[15]

Both Mattie and Angus were such prominent members of the community that James's birth put them in increased danger of being discovered by the authorities. This left Angus in a quandary. He did not dare visit Mattie and his children very often for fear of disclosing where she was hiding. She even talked about moving to Mexico to avoid arrest. In early November 1890 both Mattie and Elizabeth were ill and "in a dangerous condition." Angus recorded: "I visited Martha and found my little Elizabeth worse. I prayed with her and we joined in laying hands upon her after I had anointed. I then again knelt by the side of our little sufferer in company of her mother when I poured out my soul in prayer to God that he would permit His Angels to watch over my loved ones in this affliction, and tore myself away."[16] Shortly after, Mattie chose to take the children to San Francisco, where they found a boarding house at 21 Franklin Street.[17]

Mattie was bitter at having to once more suffer the financial blow of leaving her thriving practice in order to keep Angus out of prison and herself out of the witness chair. Elizabeth reflected that bitterness years later when she related a story undoubtedly told to her by Mattie: "When she left to go into exile to San Francisco, she left 29 confinement cases that she had beds prepared for. Some of

12. Replogle Letters, May 5, 1890.

13. Angus M. Cannon, Journals, May 19, 1890, MS 1200, Church History Library, Salt Lake City, Utah.

14. Angus M. Cannon, Journals, May 18, 1890.

15. Angus M. Cannon, Journals, May 20, 1890.

16. Angus M. Cannon, Journals, Nov. 7, 1890.

17. Nichols, "History of Elizabeth Cannon Porter McCrimmon," 6.

these she was unable to notify and they never forgave her."[18] It may not have been quite that extreme, but Mattie did express the fear of having lost friends in a non-extant letter to Angus.

The Manifesto, signaling that the church was renouncing polygamy, was signed in September 1890, but still Mattie remained in San Francisco. We do not know why; the extant letters give no clue. Perhaps she enjoyed the sea air or wanted to irritate Angus just a little. Or perhaps she suspected that the troubles were not over and did not feel safe returning immediately. As it turned out, she was correct to be wary. On April 15, 1892, Abraham Cannon recorded in his journal: "A little riffle of excitement was caused by the receiving of word that the deputy-marshals intended to make a search tonight for Mattie Paul Hughes, Uncle Angus' wife, who has just returned from California. Messengers were sent to the city to have her removed, and all went along thereafter in good order."[19]

Mattie resumed her medical practice when she returned to Salt Lake City from her second exile.[20] With its two separate entrances, her home looked like a duplex, as it served as her office and residence. Mattie paid a series of hired girls to cook and stay with the children. But the girls never stayed long, and in between each, the children were taken care of by "strangers," as Elizabeth described them. In emergencies, Elizabeth and James were sent to Grandmother Paul. (James P. Paul had died in 1891.) Despite her mother working long hours, Elizabeth recalls that Mattie "put our interests above everything." On Saturday nights they would go swimming and stop at the drug store for hot beef tea. Although the children were well cared for, one cousin recalls that "meals were irregular and things 'hung loose.'"[21]

Sometimes with Angus, but more often with friends, Mattie continued to have an active social life and often attended the theater. One of her closest friends was Amelia Folsom Young, who had acted

18. Elizabeth Cannon McCrimmon to Clair Noall, Feb. 13, 1938, Special Collections, J. Willard Marriott Library, University of Utah, Salt Lake City.

19. Abraham H. Cannon, Diary, Apr. 15, 1892, Church History Library, Salt Lake City, Utah.

20. See paragraph (no title) announcing the reopening of her medical office, in *Woman's Exponent*, Oct. 15, 1892, 59.

21. Ober, "History of Elizabeth Rachel Cannon Porter McCrimmon," 6, 7, 8.

as Brigham Young's principal hostess until his death in 1877. The two attended first nights at the Salt Lake Theater where they sat in a loge in the dress circle. Amelia took Mattie buggy riding and Mattie "lent her our ladders and the daily paper."[22]

Mattie continued to hurt financially, scrambling to find the means to support her children. The situation was not new: Angus had long been in precarious financial straits, trying to support six families. Mattie recognized that it was difficult for him: "When I say I sympathize with you financially I am sincere—as I know how it feels—as I too am menaced with a debt that threatens to [take my] home and all our belongings." Her letters to Angus deteriorated into short requests for money and services: to pay her "girl," for train fare, to pay the vegetable man, to get a coat for James, and to pay the carpenter.[23]

Mattie's practice was growing again, and along with it, an interest in politics. But she would never again be that young woman pursuing her goals with abandon, full of boundless energy, brimming with appetite for new adventures. She was now thirty-nine years old and often depressed. But even in the midst of depression, she knew she had not really given up. She wrote to Barbara in August 1887: "I feel that the spark of ambition is not yet dead within, but smolders, ready to burst into flame when the legitimate opportunity presents itself."[24] And indeed, when the opportunity came, she regrouped and began what would be a groundbreaking career in politics.

---

22. McCrimmon, "We Knew Amelia Young," 1, 4. Copy in my possession.

23. For example, see her letter to Angus written from San Francisco on February 4, 1892, in which she details her expenses and her despair that she cannot provide for her children as she wants. Angus M. Cannon collection, MS 1200, box 10, fd. 4, Church History Library, Salt Lake City, Utah.

24. Replogle Letters, Aug. 6, 1887.

CHAPTER SEVEN

SUFFRAGE AND STATEHOOD

Along with both California and New Mexico, Utah Territory was working to become a state. Plural marriage, however, was a sticking point. The Mormons refused to give up a practice they considered revealed by God; the United States refused to admit a territory where polygamy was practiced. The federal government gradually ratcheted up measures designed to force church members to abandon polygamy, culminating in the threat of the government taking over church properties. In the 1890 Manifesto, issued by church president Wilford Woodruff, the practice of polygamy was banned (although, as the *Woman's Exponent* pointed out, the belief itself was not abandoned). And the main thrust of church politics grew beyond countering the various anti-polygamy measures, focusing instead on obtaining statehood.

Mormon women mobilized not just to obtain statehood but to regain the vote. Their main argument rested on the fact that one of their rights had been revoked: "As we [women] in Utah have held the franchise, we feel most keenly on the subject."[1]

Mormon women were not neophytes in either thinking about or acting on the subject of female suffrage. The subtitle of the *Woman's Exponent* read: "The Rights of the Women of Zion and the Rights of the Women of All Nations." They participated in their local organizations and as often as possible in national meetings. Susan B. Anthony and other leaders of the woman suffrage movement traveled to Salt Lake City several times, and Mattie, who was rising in

---

1. "Lehi W.S.A.," *Woman's Exponent*, Jan. 15, 1890, 129.

importance in both the local and national movements, made their acquaintance.[2]

At the Woman Suffrage Association of Utah meeting held on April 11, 1889, Mattie was a featured speaker. "To make men and women nobler, or purer, or more intelligent, is the object of every worthy enterprise, political and social. But laudable goals are not sufficient." She described the past forty years of the woman suffrage movement as "vacillating, complicated and disconnected," for "there must be a combination of motive and work, a blending of intellect and emotion, a strong desire with a firm hand, a righteous purpose with competent skill to accomplish any permanent good, or to carry to success any needed reform." She contrasted the earlier state of women's rights, when "to be born a female was to become a plaything and a slave," with her day, when "in the best and most powerful circles, woman is the peer of the noblest man." Only the right to vote was still lacking, and Utah women, who once had that right, were therefore "justified in appealing to the nation to regain that which rightly belongs to us."

In this speech, Mattie decried the idea of a "privileged class either of sex, wealth, or descent" but declared that "all persons should have the legal right to be the equal of every other." She made her own prediction of how society would look once women had equal rights with men before the law: "there will doubtless then be some drunken, brutal husbands, some parsimonious and contemptible heads of families, fraud and wrong-doing, aching heads and aching hearts, perhaps as many as now, but the skirts of the law will be clean … and woman will then stand where she rightfully belongs, on an equal platform with man before the law."

Yet in her own schema of society, women themselves were, in effect, divided into classes. For Mattie, the "classes" were the educated and the uneducated. She made ample use of this "lower class" herself, hiring "girls" to cook and clean and tend her children so that she was free to practice medicine and politics. She never explicitly says that some women should be out in the world and some should stay home, but she remarks over and over that keeping house saps a woman's intellectual

---

2. Shari Siebers Crall, "'Something More': A Biography of Martha Hughes Cannon," (honors thesis, Brigham Young University, 1985), 65.

power and that she should therefore be freed from such menial chores. Obviously, equality could never be applied across the board to encompass all women—some would clearly be needed to keep the houses and the children of the women who were taking on more and more of the roles that had previously been the domain of men.[3]

These were not new ideas. Shortly after her marriage, Mattie waxed eloquent on how keeping house hinders advancement, writing to Barbara Reprogle: "After all, [marriage] is the true state of womanhood. Neither if properly managed should it interfere with her true advancement, in whatever sphere she might cast her talents—'Tis not the bringing of noble spirits into the world—to me, a woman's brightest glory—that dwarfs talent and retards her intellectual advancement, but it is the multiplicity of household drudgery which *only belongs to servants*—and the conformity to the vile customs of modern Society."[4] It is interesting how Mattie, always a vocal advocate for women, nonetheless accepted a two-tiered valuation of women: those who should have the opportunity to advance and those who should make that advancement possible by taking over household and childcare duties.

At the same time that Mattie advocated equal rights in the law, she recognized that many inequalities stemmed not so much from unjust laws but "more from custom and fashion." She challenged women to get educated and separate themselves from that which held them back, to no longer be slaves to fashion and frivolities, and to cease ruining their minds by reading "trashy novels." Invoking her medical knowledge, she said, "It is a shame, even a crime under divine laws for a woman to lace herself into clothing, which makes a consumptive suicide of herself, and deteriorates the physical being of her offspring." She concluded her speech with a dramatic plea undoubtedly made in the ringing tones she learned at the National School and for which her oratory was known: "May the day be

---

3. These ideas were laid out clearly in an 1896 interview with "Annie Laurie," "Our Woman Senator. The First to Be Elected in America," *San Francisco Examiner*, Nov. 8, 1896, reprinted in *Salt Lake Herald*, Nov. 11, 1896. "Annie Laurie" was the pseudonym of Mrs. Winnifred Black, who was, interestingly, opposed to female suffrage.

4. Letters to Barbara Replogle Atkinson, Martha H. Cannon collection, 1883–1912, MS 8867, Oct. 2, 1884, Church History Library, Church of Jesus Christ of Latter-day Saints, Salt Lake City.

hastened when we will not only have our rights, but also know them, and *knowing dare maintain.*"[5]

Although Mattie and her contemporaries were agitating for women's rights, we must be careful to not ascribe to them qualities of proto-twenty-first-century feminists. We should not assume they completely shared our concept of women as fully equal to men—able to take on any role a man does. Mattie was a progressive woman for her time, but despite her groundbreaking actions and opinions, also very much of her time: a typical Victorian/Edwardian woman.

For example, she said that some political offices were suitable for women but others were not. It was nearly impossible for her to imagine a woman in the role of a constable arresting men or as a sheriff responsible for hanging them. She makes a stark delineation between a woman taking on roles that were currently thought of as being only for men and being like a man, which would include occupations she thought inappropriate for women. As she wrote to Angus in 1886: "The more I 'spread out' after the manner of men ... the happier I am. And yet I am not a bit 'mannish.' I wouldn't be a *man* for all creation."[6]

In 1893 the women of Utah were enthusiastically preparing to participate in the Columbian Exposition in Chicago. It had been billed as bringing "all the departments of human progress into har-monious relations in a great intellectual and moral exposition." The organizers aimed to "sum up the progress of mankind in every de-partment of enlightened achievement." Twenty-seven countries and 126 organizations were represented."[7]

Utah women from each county were asked to present something representative of their area to exhibit in the Utah Pavilion and to make "the Utah building elegant and attractive."[8]

Mattie was a featured speaker. The *Exponent* of June 15, 1893,

---

5. "Woman Suffrage Meeting," *Woman's Exponent*, May 15, 1889, 190. Emphasis added.

6. Constance L. Lieber and John Sillito, eds., *Letters from Exile: The Correspondence of Martha Hughes Cannon and Angus M. Cannon, 1886–1888* (Salt Lake City: Signature Books, 1989), 8.

7. Ida Husted Harper, *The Life and Work of Susan B. Anthony Including Public Ad-dresses, Her Own Letters and Many from Her Contemporaries During Fifty Years: A Story of the Evolution of the Status of Women* (Indianapolis: Bowen–Merrill Co., 1898), 244.

8. "Editorial Notes; The Utah Room," *Woman's Exponent*, Apr. 1, 1893, 148.

recorded part of Mattie's talk.[9] The *Ashtabula News* described Mattie as "a beautiful, bright, young woman."[10] The *Chicago Record* pronounced her "one of the brightest exponents of women's cause in the United States."[11] Alice Merrill Horne, speaking at Mattie's funeral in 1932, recalled, "I saw her moving in the circles with the forward-looking women of Zion, joining in all things to advance her sisterhood."[12] Finally, Claire Wilcox Noall reported that Mattie "walked down the aisle at the meeting of the Congress, beautifully tailored in a green suit, with hat, gloves, and bag to harmonize. A love of finery had become an exacting sense of fitness." Noall's reconstruction of that talk may contain fictions and hyperbole, but it certainly sounds like Mattie: "'Utah women have known the power of the ballot! We shall enjoy the feel of that strong lever in our hands again.' Higher and higher rose her pitch as she outlined the innumerable ways in which woman's legislation might benefit public welfare. 'Let the inception of freedom through health commence with woman's voice in the local legislatures of these United States. Do what you can in the countries of Europe. Go home, my friends, and fight.'"[13]

During this time of excitement over the Chicago Exposition, which launched Mattie into the national consciousness, she had not abandoned her medical practice, although it was decidedly curtailed, both by her absences and by her reduced business hours. Advertisements in the *Exponent* show that she had restricted her practice to the "diseases of women" and had office hours only between 2:00 and 4:00 p.m.[14]

A meeting of the Assembly of Women (under the auspices of the Utah Woman Suffrage Association—WSA) held on February 3, 1894, boasted "speeches [that] were logical and eloquent and it will

---

9. "Utah Women in Chicago. Dr. Cannon's Address," *Woman's Exponent*, June 15, 1893, 170. Copied from the *Chicago Daily Tribune*, May 20, 1893.

10. "The World's Fair. Another Interesting Letter from Our Correspondent," *Woman's Exponent*, June 15, 1893, 177–78. Copied from *The Ashtabula News Journal*, May 23, 1893.

11. "Woman's Great Forum," *Chicago Record*, May 15, 1893.

12. Alice Merrill Horne, speech delivered at the funeral of Martha Hughes Cannon, July 14, 1932, Salt Lake City, in Crall, "'Something More'," 66.

13. Claire Wilcox Noall, "Utah's Pioneer Women Doctors," *Improvement Era*, Mar. 1939, 181.

14. For example, see advertisement, "Dr. Mattie Hughes Cannon," *Woman's Exponent*, Jan. 15, 1893, 112.

no doubt be the means of awakening [women's] thought upon [the] subject." Mattie gave a "stirring address" which she closed with a poem which was, "thrillingly rendered." This meeting is where she gave her most celebrated talk, focusing on the fatal *Somethingmore*. The *Exponent* thought the speech so important that it was printed in full in the April 1, 1894, issue.[15]

First, she chided her fellow Utahns. "In the enrollment of members in the suffrage cause Utah stands second in the United States [to New York State] ... and while we rank among the first in numbers, we bring up the rear in the matter of enthusiasm."

Then she chided the so-called privileged class of women—those "who were doing, comparatively, quite well under the existing system, with incentives to hang onto a system that privileged them"—who were active in the anti-suffrage campaign. These women "were generally urban, often the daughters and-or wives of well-to-do men of business, banking or politics. They were also quite likely to be involved in philanthropic or 'reform' work that hewed to traditional gender norms." They were "concerned with societal disruptions" that would alter or harm the mother's established role in society and thereby lose existing privileges. These women's status was a result of the status quo—and they did not want that to change.[16]

Mattie then related the story of a peri in Ormudz who loved precious jewels.[17] However, there was one jewel, rivaling the sun in brightness, that she had been unable to obtain: the *Somethingmore*. Only by possessing that gem did she believe she would be happy. Finally, she got the jewel, set it in her crown, and flew off to impress her neighbors. But the fiery blaze of the jewel scorched her wings

---

15. See "Editorial Notes," *Woman's Exponent*, Feb. 1 and 15, 1894, 92; and "A Woman's Assembly [Concluded]: Address by M. Hughes Cannon, M.D.," *Woman's Exponent*, Apr. 1, 1894, 113–14.

16. See www.npr.org/sections/npr-history-dept: "American Women Who Were Anti-Suffragettes," Oct. 22, 2015. Two celebrated anti-suffragists were Josephine Jewell Dodge, whose husband was from a powerful New York family, and Kate Douglas Wiggins, a popular children's book author. Dodge was worried about "women's integration into the 'corrupt' world of party politics," and Wiggins was quoted as saying she would have "woman strong enough to keep just a trifle in the background, for the limelight never makes anything grow."

17. A "peri" is a fairy in Persian mythology, while Ormuzd (Mattie spelled it wrong and turned it into a place name) represents the first-born of beings.

and the ground around her until she fell dead of suffocation. The moral of the story, according to one prominent opponent of woman's suffrage, was that women already had all the equal rights they required—and called the ballot the fatal *Somethingmore* that would eventually destroy them were they to obtain it.

Mattie scoffed at that idea, declaring "This ... might do to tell the women of the East who have never had the franchise, but not for the women of Utah who exercised this privilege for seventeen years without scorching a single wing."[18]

She detailed some of the anti-suffragists' reasons against suffrage: it would destroy women's purity and only bad women would vote; they would only vote as their husbands do, showing little independent thought; or, if they did vote independently, there would be domestic discord. In a speech given in mid-August 1895, Mattie declared that there was no truth in the argument that "when [a woman] dabbles in politics, she neglects her home and family [and that] the true woman cannot be induced to forget her duties by reason of political activity any more than the true man can be influenced to fail to perform his part of the work."[19] The audience applauded vigorously, as her audiences often did. A few days later she spoke at a Democratic rally. Her speech "kept the audience in almost continual applause. It was full of wit and characteristic humor."[20]

Ever pragmatic and willing to speak her mind, Mattie also stated that she doubted "the privilege of voting and the holding of political offices by women [was] going to do all that the zealous advocates of woman's suffrage now claim." "If women are granted the privilege to vote, it is not going by any means to sweep away all existing wrong in the world ... there will be fraud and wrong, but the skirts of the law will be clean."[21]

The culmination of Utah suffrage efforts came at the Utah Territorial WSA convention held in the Salt Lake City and County Building on March 18, 1895. A committee, which included Mattie, was formed to draft a document to give to the Utah Constitutional Convention,

---

18. "A Woman's Assembly," *Woman's Exponent*, Apr. 1, 1894, 113–14.

19. "Enthusiastic Democratic Meeting in the Fifteenth Ward," *Salt Lake Herald*, Aug. 16, 1895.

20. "Enthusiastic Democratic Meeting."

21. "A Woman's Assembly," *Woman's Exponent*, Apr. 1, 1894, 114.

then in session. The *Exponent* reports that the "committee retired for 5 minutes and returned with the memorial, which was adopted and signed." The document was read aloud to the convention and then it was referred to the committee on elections and suffrage. It read, in part: "We, your memorialists speak in their names and in behalf of the women of Utah [and] herewith present the woman's cause. It is a matter of congratulation that in these closing years of the nineteenth century the cause of woman can, without the stigma of partisanship, be laid before a body of chosen men ordained to the work of creating a new sovereignty within the galaxy of states; as an equal member of the indissoluble Union. The men of Utah, in their respective political parties have with equal unanimity, said that women shall be accorded equal rights and privileges of citizenship, that sex distinction shall no longer be a ban and a bar to equal opportunity with men."[22]

Finally, on May 1, 1895, the *Exponent* reported: "When the vote was taken it stood sixty-nine to thirty-two, and the section as originally formulated by the majority committee on Elections and Suffrage goes into the Constitution of the New State giving women equal political privileges with men."[23] Susan B. Anthony, who had been watching closely, wrote a joyful letter to Emmeline B. Wells, which was reprinted in the *Salt Lake Tribune:* "Oh, how good this little item makes me feel! Just to think that you and all of the dear women of Utah will be full-fledged citizens possessed of the right to vote on every question on equal terms with men."[24]

On Wednesday, May 8, after sixty-six days in session, Utah's constitution finally went "before the legal voters of the Territory." The *Exponent* expressed little doubt as to the final result.[25]

All that remained was for the women to register to vote. The *Salt Lake Herald* duly reported: "Registrar Cowley of the Second Precinct" "took time by the forelock" and opened up voter registration to the women of the territory. Mattie was first in line.[26]

---

22. "Equal Suffrage in the Constitution," *Woman's Exponent*, May 1, 1895, 260.

23. "Conferences and Conventions," *Woman's Exponent,* Apr. 15, 1895, 252.

24. "Susan B. Contratulates [*sic*]," *Salt Lake Tribune*, Dec. 29, 1895.

25. "The Convention Adjourned," *Woman's Exponent*, May 15, 1895, 269.

26. "Examiner Has Opened Up. Women Are Registered," *Salt Lake Herald*, Aug. 8, 1895.

CHAPTER EIGHT

SENATOR CANNON

As Utahns prepared themselves for the first general election under the new state constitution, there was much rejoicing that both men and women could vote—and presumably much astonishment when the Republication and Democratic slates were revealed. Angus was a candidate for state senator on the Republican ticket and Mattie on the Democratic.

In the "Annie Laurie" interview, Mattie explained the situation like this: "Well, this year we got suffrage, and the party [Democratic] thought there ought to be a lady in the senate, and a committee came and asked me if I would run and I said 'yes.' I went to the nominating convention as a delegate. My name was offered as a candidate and I was duly nominated. Then I went home and congratulated Mr. Cannon on his nomination."[1]

L. R. Letcher gave the speech at the Democratic Party convention nominating Mattie as a senatorial candidate: "My candidate is a graduate of two medical colleges, but yet a womanly woman. If nominated she will be elected and will go to the legislature with the sole idea of performing her duty to her constituents. ... Her name is Dr. Mattie Hughes Cannon and I dare any man to vote against her."[2]

Although the press cast the coming election as one in which Angus and Mattie were running against each other, that was not the case. They were each one in a slate of a total of five candidates running at large. Indeed, if Mattie were to be thought of as running

---

1. Annie Laurie Black, "Our Woman Senator," *San Francisco Examiner*, Nov. 8, 1896, as reprinted in *Salt Lake Herald*, Nov. 11, 1896.
2. "Choice of Democrats," *Salt Lake Tribune*, Sep. 20, 1896.

against someone in particular, that someone would have been Emmeline B. Wells, who was added to the Republican ticket so that they, too, had a female candidate. But it was Mattie and Angus who garnered the biggest headlines though both of them might have won or both might have lost.

The local press was alternately amused and outraged. Democrats, only half seriously, proposed a public debate between the married couple. "What would draw a bigger crowd, to whom the truths of democracy might be expounded, than the prospect of a public verbal set-to between Dr. Mattie Hughes Cannon and her husband, Angus M. Cannon?"[3] There was no public debate although the possibility continued to be bandied about in the press. When the *Salt Lake Herald*, staunchly Democratic, wrote that Mattie would be a better senator than Angus, the *Salt Lake Tribune*, just as staunchly Republican, retorted, "We do not see anything for Angus M. to do but to either go home and break a bouquet over Mrs. Cannon's head, to show his superiority, or to go up to the *Herald* office and break a chair over the head of the man who wrote that disturber of domestic peace."[4]

The election also attracted the attention of the national press, including the *St. Paul (Minnesota) Globe*, which reported on October 25, 1896, that Mr. Cannon, "a four-ply polygamist" [i.e., had four wives], was running against his wife.[5] As with most of the other journalists, this reporter either did not know or ignored the fact that Angus had six wives. The *Morning Times* of Washington, DC, noted that other papers had printed photographs of "this lady" and concluded that "she was, indeed, rather nice-looking, and all of the accounts have it that she is very bright."[6] One correspondent for the *New York Times* wrote a surprisingly measured and undramatic article compared with the more sensational slant of most: "One of the most interesting advocates of woman suffrage in Utah is Dr. Martha Hughes Cannon. ... She was one of the plural wives of Angus M. Cannon ... but showed her intense independence by declining to follow the political convictions of her husband, who is one of the staunchest Republicans in the

3. "Joint Debate Proposed," *Salt Lake Tribune*, Oct. 12, 1896.

4. Jean Bickmore White, "Gentle Persuaders: Utah's First Women Legislators," *Utah Historical Quarterly* 38, no. 1 (Winter 1970): 33.

5. "Women in Politics," *St. Paul Globe*, Oct. 25, 1896.

6. "Women for Senators," *Morning Times* (Washington, DC), Jan. 13, 1897.

State." However, in the same article, the reporter expressed (erroneously) the assumption that "the operation of the anti-polygamy laws caused her to separate from her husband."[7]

The major issue in the 1896 presidential election was the free and unlimited coinage of silver—the platform of the national Democratic Party, represented by their presidential candidate, William Jennings Bryan.[8] Most Utahans were firmly in that camp, feeling it would help the country emerge from the depressed economy of the mid-1890s and stimulate mining and agriculture in Utah. The issue split the Republican Party in Utah, greatly contributing to their loss in the election. All five Democratic candidates were elected; all five Republican candidates lost. Utah returned the most votes, 82.7 percent, for Bryan.[9]

Emmeline was "devastated" to have lost, along with all other Republican candidates. But she summed up the whole process with humor and insight: "What an experience this has been for me. It has been very exciting for me and quite new too—we are all beginners."[10]

Angus was reportedly "sweating blood" on election night as he waited for the returns,[11] even though the *Salt Lake Tribune* predicted he would win: "There will be another Senator Cannon [the reference is to the US Senator from Utah, Frank J. Cannon] in Utah after Tuesday next. The Cannon on the Democratic ticket, however, is not

---

7. "Women Office Seekers," *New York Times*, Nov. 1, 1896, Sunday supplement. Shari Crall comments: "This article is generally accurate and gives an interesting insight into the national response to both the members of the Church and Martha Hughes Cannon's election" (Shari Siebers Crall, "'Something More': A Biography of Martha Hughes Cannon," (honors thesis, Brigham Young University, 1985), 98).

8. Mattie's daughter Elizabeth, according to Shari Siebers Crall, claims Mattie "gave speeches all over the west alongside the brilliant orator and Democratic presidential nominee, William Jennings Bryan, for the cause of free silver." See McCrimmon, "First Woman Senator," 8, and Crall, "'Something More,'" 71. Although it is documented that Mattie gave speeches in favor of silver, I can find no evidence that she toured with Bryan. See, for example, "One of His Wives Beat Him," *Xenia (OH) Daily Gazette*, Nov. 9, 1896. It is amusing to note that Mattie is called "Agnes M. Cannon" in some of the articles from non-Utah papers.

9. See Allan Kent Powell, "Election in the State of Utah," *Utah Historical Encyclopedia*, www.uen.org/utah_history_encyclopedia under the Elections heading.

10. Emmeline B. Wells, Diary, Aug. 26, 1895, in Carol Cornwall Madsen, *An Advocate for Women: The Public Life of Emmeline B. Wells, 1870–1920*, Biographies in Latter-day Saint History (Provo, Utah: Brigham Young University Press, 2006), 340.

11. Quoted in White, "Gentle Persuaders," 33.

the one who is to win legislative honors. They are to be conferred on her husband Angus M. Cannon."[12] We may imagine him in anguish, perhaps tempered with some anger, when Mattie bested him, but in typical Angus-fashion, publicly at least, he took a pragmatic approach to his loss. In a letter to a prominent acquaintance in New York, shortly after the election, Angus wrote: "My wife aspired to be a State Senator and it looks as if she will get here while I planned to get there but failed. Notwithstanding this I am not going to separate from my wife but will try and keep as near as I can and *be happy*."[13] In at least one interview, Mattie said that Angus, in fact, wanted *her* to win: "He met me the day before the poll and said, 'Now how do you expect to come out girl?' I really believe he wished me to win."[14]

The national press had a heyday when it was made known that Mattie had not only dared to run against her husband, but had, in fact, defeated him. Over the next two years, most national newspapers carried stories highlighting Mattie's election and Angus's defeat. Most had great fun with the fact that a plural wife had bested her husband, but none more so than the *New York Mail and Express*, which wondered whether Mattie had gotten the votes of Angus's other wives, "giving Mr. Cannon an exceedingly painful uncertainty as to his status in his own household."[15] *The Evening Bulletin* (Maysville, Kentucky) wrote that Mattie was famous as the first woman who was ever sent to a state senate, noting that she had served two years and had two to go. The story recounts her education and her role as the "sixth wife" of Angus Munn Cannon. "In the political campaign for state senator President Cannon ran against his wife, Dr. Martha Hughes Cannon, and was defeated, as all the world knows. She represented the silver democracy and received a handsome majority of votes."[16] Mattie received about 3,000 more votes than Angus.

12. "Salt Lake Delegation—Entire Republican Ticket to be Elected—Merits of Candidates," *Salt Lake Tribune*, Nov. 2, 1896.

13. Angus M. Cannon to Judge J. McNalley, Dec. 19, 1896, in Angus M. Cannon, Letterbooks, MS 1200, Church History Library, Church of Jesus Christ of Latter-day Saints, Salt Lake City.

14. David A. Shannon, ed., *Beatrice Webb's American Diary, 1896* (Madison: University of Wisconsin Press, 1960), 132.

15. The Woman Senator," *Buffalo Morning Express and Illustrated Buffalo Express*, Dec. 13, 1896.

16. "Dr. Martha Hughes Cannon," *The Evening Bulletin* (Maysville, KY), Jan. 14, 1898.

Other reports were similar, capitalizing on the fact that Mattie was a polygamous wife. The *Detroit Free Press* wrote: "Mrs. Cannon believes in polygamy, and is a victim of it, if victim she can be called when she can whip her lord and master at the polls."[17] Another newspaper reported that Mattie had replied in her usual lively and direct fashion to the slur that as a plural wife, she was only one quarter a wife: "[Then I am] only ¼ the slave one wife is."[18] One Detroit newspaper, in a curious aside, conceded that after besting her husband, Mattie was "not conceited."[19]

The female candidates in the race for state senator received most of the press. However, there were also four women running for the House. Of the four, two Democrats—Sarah E. Anderson of Weber County and Eurethe LaBarthe[20] (not an LDS Church member) of Salt Lake County—were elected.

Utah's second legislature convened on January 11, 1897. The *Salt Lake Tribune* reported that Mattie was late arriving and found bouquets of roses on her desk. Her great-granddaughter Arline Brady says that her desk was always covered with flowers.[21] Mattie explained it this way: "Since I don't attend the stag parties nor smoke the cigars, people send me flowers instead."[22] Her daughter Elizabeth remembered, "During both winter sessions of the legislature, her desk in the Senate chamber and our own home were a mass of hothouse roses and other flowers that bloom out of Season." Mattie was admired by the other senators, as witnessed by the inscriptions in her autograph book. One, by Thomas M. Evans, reads: "Mrs. Martha Hughes Cannon / The first lady ever elected to the high office of State Senator in the Great American Union / My kindest regards."[23]

---

17. "Woman in the Senate," *Detroit Free Press*, Nov. 17, 1896.

18. "A Fair Polygamist," *Atchison (KS) Daily Globe*, Dec. 1, 1896.

19. "The First Woman Senator," *Daily Inter Ocean* (Chicago, IL), Nov. 29, 1896.

20. The *New York Times* pointed out that La Barthe was one of "the non-Mormon element. ... She is a bright, active, well-educated woman, who has one grown son, and who therefore has leisure for politics, for which she has a natural aptitude and liking" ("Women Office Seekers," Nov. 1, 1896).

21. Arline Brady, interview with the author, Feb. 2, 2012; also Elizabeth Cannon McCrimmon to Claire Noall, Mar. 12, 1938, Special Collections, J. Willard Marriott Library, University of Utah, Salt Lake City.

22. Elizabeth Cannon McCrimmon, undated, untitled manuscript, 18, in my possession.

23. Autograph book, in possession of Arline Brady.

Elizabeth wrote that the flowers were sent by many different people, including the young Senator D. H. Peery, Jr., a rich playboy from Ogden. "Mother wept when he died soon after."[24]

The origins of Mattie's autograph album, as well as a favorable assessment of Mattie's work as a senator for the first few months, was published by *The Evening Times* of Washington, DC: "Mrs. Cannon has been scrutinized with the sharpest anxiety by both her friends and her enemies. If she had been inconsistent, if she had allowed some mood of unreason to influence her course, if she had been even suspected of yielding to the persuasions of the lobbyist, the world would have heard of it quickly enough." The article became flippant as it described the gift of the autograph book: "[The other senators] clubbed together and bought her a present. Perhaps they hadn't done such a thing since they were boys at school as to club all together and buy a present for a lady. And the gift they selected goes to confirm this theory. It was an embossed leather autograph album." The reporter may have thought the gift somewhat juvenile, but Mattie cherished it and filled it with autographs and testimonials from those with whom she worked in the senate.[25]

Emmeline, working behind the scenes rather than as the senator she had hoped to be, spent time helping Mattie get the information she needed as she pushed forward her proposed legislation, writing on December 9, 1897, "I went through piles of manuscript and printed matter to get material for Dr. M. H. Cannon to write up. Spent most of the afternoon talking and explaining things to her."[26]

Mattie, even though her focus was on public health, had also to contend with the demeaning attitudes and low expectations expressed towards the first women legislators. Beatrice Webb, the noted British socialist and reformer who came to Salt Lake City in June 1898 to interview Mattie, was condescending. She described Mattie's house and office, at #11 South First West Street, as "a little wooden villa overshadowed by trees."

---

24. Elizabeth Cannon Porter [McCrim.non] to Claire Noall, Feb. 13, 1938.

25. "To a Lady Senator," *Evening Times* (Washington, DC), Mar. 23, 1897, 4. The autograph book is in the possession of her great-granddaughter Arline Brady.

26. Emmeline B. Wells, Diary, Dec. 9, 1897, in Diary Typescripts, 1844–1920, MSS 1407, L. Tom Perry Special Collections, Harold B. Lee Library, Brigham Young University, Provo.

Webb described Mattie herself as "a sprightly pleasant-looking little person with energetic gait and decided manner." After discussing what she understood of LDS beliefs and polygamy, Webb summed up Mattie as "such a self-respectful vigourous pure-minded little soul: sensitive yet unself-conscious, indiscreet yet loyal. She had no training for the political career she had chosen, and I suspect her medical knowledge was as fragmentary as her economics. As a citizen I should doubt her wisdom as a legislator—and as a patient I certainly should not trust her skill in diagnosing my case. But as a friend I should rely on her warm sympathy and freedom from the meaner motives of life."[27]

The most celebrated and extensive article about Mattie the senator was by Annie Laurie, the pen name of Mrs. Orlow (Winnifred) Black of San Francisco, who was against woman suffrage. She traveled to Salt Lake City and conducted a long interview with the new senator.[28]

In the interview, Laurie asked questions about polygamy, woman suffrage, prohibition, and how Mattie came to run for senator. Her descriptions of Mattie and her home give us insight into the woman. And her reproduction of Mattie's sometimes surprising and sometimes incomprehensible opinions is alternately illuminating and amusing.

"Martha Hughes Cannon, the senator, is a doctor by profession. She lives in a neat little red brick house ... [and] has a little girl, eleven years old and a little boy, seven years old. She is between 30 and 35 to look at [she was thirty-nine], and she is a clear-skinned, slender, trim little woman, well-groomed and fresh, with brown hair plentifully sprinkled with gray and a pair of brilliant, alert hazel eyes. She has little bits of thin hands and little bits of slim feet, and she wears good clothes of a quiet unobtrusive kind. She has a clear voice and a good serviceable vocabulary, and she is perfectly free from self-consciousness of any sort."

Mattie emphasized her loyalty to the Democratic Party as she described her campaign: "I worked pretty hard. I studied up on all the questions of the campaign and I made a lot of speeches. I did not do any personal work, talking to people myself, and why they ought

---

27. David A. Shannon, ed., *Beatrice Webb's American Diary, 1898*, (Madison: University of Wisconsin Press, 1963), 29 June [1898], 130–35.

28. "Our Woman Senator," *Salt Lake Herald*, Nov. 11, 1896.

to vote for me, I mean. I just stayed right with my party and spoke for that, and on election day I went to the polls and voted. Then I went and attended to my patients."

When asked what her goals as a senator were, Mattie replied that she would focus on health and educational issues, because "women are good ones for those things." She claimed that women active in politics would both help the women and purify politics. Her reasoning is unusual, as she pointed to the previous status of women, which she equated to slavery: "Women are better than men. Slaves are always better than their masters. A slave learns obedience and self-control and unselfishness. That's why women will do the world of politics good. They have been slaves so long. They will teach some of the slavish virtues."

When asked for her opinion on prohibition, it was clear that she did not agree with her friend Barbara Reprogle, who was a noted temperance campaigner: "On the saloon question I stand with my party. Prohibition does not prohibit. ... I don't believe anyone who has lived in Europe much can scare up such a terrifically strong hatred of the demon rum."[29] Mattie clearly moderated her opinion in order to stand with the Democratic Party, not mentioning her distress in England over her aunt's drunkenness and how it caused the aunt to mistreat her own children.[30]

Naturally, Laurie and most of her readers were intensely interested in Mattie's views on polygamy, which Mattie slanted to emphasize the intelligence of Utah women: "Of course it is all at an end now. But I think and the women of Utah think with me that we were better off in the state of polygamy. Sixty percent of the voters of this state are women. ... Oh, we control the state."

What followed next was a somewhat comic exchange that left the interviewer flummoxed. Mattie said, "I don't want [women] to run for unseemly offices. Take the governor, for instance, that's too mannish altogether. I can't bear a mannish woman or a mannish man either. By mannishness I mean, you perceive, not an inherent quality,

---

29. "Utah's New Senator. Mrs. Martha Hughes Cannon Defeats Her Husband at the Polls," *Minneapolis Journal*, Nov. 20, 1896.

30. Constance L. Lieber and John Sillito, eds., *Letters from Exile, The Correspondence of Martha Hughes Cannon and Angus M. Cannon, 1886–1888* (Salt Lake City: Signature Books, 1989), 12.

but an assumption, a sticking out of the elbows and a raising of the head and a strutting." Laurie described the scene: "Mrs. Cannon pointed her elbows and raised her head and began to strut, thought better of it, and sank into her chair." Mattie continued: "That is as offensive to me in a man as in a woman. All the best men I know are ladylike and all the best women I know are gentlemanly. You catch my idea, I perceive." Laurie did not understand, and wrote that she gave a "perfidious nod," indicating to the reader that the nod should not be taken as agreement.

Mattie was also pressed to give her opinion of women working in the home, of polygamy, of politics during the Millennium, and of the potential progress of men and women. "Will there be legislatures and ward politics and women senators [during the Millennium]?" Mattie sidestepped the question: "Oh, you are too literal. Women must not be too literal. Men [Mattie's voice reportedly took on a "platform ring" and her eyes were "pathetic"] are wedded to the present; women are promised to the future." Laurie argued: "But you are not promised to the future. You have arrived." "Ah," Mattie replied, "the first woman senator. I hadn't thought of it in that light. I do seem to be a sort of milestone, don't I? Well, I will have to try to live up to my privileges."[31]

Mattie did not hesitate to introduce bills focused on public health. The *Times-Picayune* of New Orleans reported on one of her early efforts: "Mrs. Martha Hughes Cannon, the only woman in the Utah senate has introduced a bill for the better protection of the health of women clerks, and it has passed both houses."[32] In fact, Mattie introduced three bills in the first session of the second legislature:

1. *An Act Providing for the Compulsory Education of Deaf, Dumb, and Blind Children (S.B. 22).* The education of children who—at the time—did not attend public schools, was a subject Mattie was familiar with, as she had been appointed to the board of the Deaf and Dumb Institute in early 1896.[33]

2. *An Act Creating a State Board of Health and Defining Its Duties (S.B. 27).* This was her greatest and most long-lasting achievement.

31. All quotations are from "Our Woman Senator," *Salt Lake Herald*, Nov. 11, 1896.
32. "Women's Reading," *Times-Picayune* (New Orleans, LA), Apr. 5, 1897.
33. "Passing Events," *Woman's Exponent*, Apr. 15, 1896.

The act established a seven-member State Board of Health, to which Mattie was appointed. The board was charged with the responsibility to encourage the establishment of local boards of health and to improve disease control, sanitation, and the water supply. The board was also responsible for compiling the first statutes aimed at effecting a statewide campaign improving public health.[34] Establishing the State Board of Health and turning it into a functioning entity was frustrating because it was breaking new ground. Local officials were apathetic and slow to organize local boards of health. It became evident that supplemental legislation was needed to strengthen the original act and garner public support for the law that prohibited children with contagious diseases from attending school.[35] Reinforcing the establishment of the State Board of Health and addressing specific problems in public health were largely taken care of in the third legislature, in 1899.[36] Mattie also introduced acts to define quarantine rules, provide for burial permits, promote the protection of water supplies, and establish rules for the inspection of school buildings.[37]

3. *An Act to Protect the Health of Women and Girl Employees (S.B. 31)*. This act, which the New Orleans's newspaper reported on, was in response to a female saleslady who showed Mattie how women clerks rested by sitting on open cupboards and dresser drawers. This bill required employers to provide places for their female employees to rest when they were not helping customers.[38] The legislators who passed the bill considered it progressive legislation.[39]

Besides amending and expanding the bill that established the State Board of Health, Mattie introduced a bill during the third legislature mandating that a hospital building for the Utah State

34. Jean Bickmore White, "Martha H. Cannon," in Vicky Burgess–Olson, ed., *Sister Saints* (Provo, Utah: Brigham Young University Press, 1978), 390; and White, "Gentle Persuaders," 45. White writes that "the act became part of the revised statutes that were compiled by a special commission and provided the basis for a statewide attack on problems of sanitation and contagious disease."

35. "Report of the State Board of Heath," *Utah Public Documents,* 1897–98, Sec. 22.

36. "State Health Board," *Salt Lake Herald,* Apr. 21, 1898, 5.

37. White, "Gentle Persuaders," 45; "Report of the State Board of Health," *Utah Public Documents,* 1889–1900, Sec. 22.

38. Elizabeth Cannon McCrimmon, in Crall, "'Something More,'" 81.

39. White, "Gentle Persuaders," 48.

School for the Deaf and Dumb be built.[40] Mattie remained on the board of that school until she was appointed to the State Board of Health in 1898.

The only bill Mattie introduced that was not passed was State Bill 37, which stipulated that the dangers of alcohol and narcotics be taught in the public schools. It was passed by the Senate but defeated in the House.

Alice Merrill Horne, who was elected to the House for the third legislature, worked with Mattie in advancing legislation "that [was] dear to our hearts and that has been beneficial to citizens of this state, having something to do with Public Health and Sanitation." Horne described Mattie as a "competent person, a just legislator, a parliamentarian, a gracious, kindly, beautiful woman, a lover of good, a chosen person. Men and women too, [take] counsel from her." She deferred to Mattie, who was older "and wise." The two women did not often speak on the floor of the legislature, but rather took their arguments to each senator and representative privately. Judge Tilman D. Johnson said: "Mrs. Horne, tell Mrs. Martha H. Cannon for me that I am converted to equal suffrage, for several of us have agreed that the women members of the Third Legislature have voted more intelligently than the men."[41]

The National American Woman Suffrage Association Convention in Washington, DC, was organized to mark the 50th year of the founding of the suffrage movement. Women from across the United States attended. According to the *Woman's Exponent*, Mattie had been given a special invitation to attend. She left Salt Lake City on February 14, 1898, and "arrived in good time (no doubt) for the opening session." She planned to speak at the convention and also at a special senate committee meeting on woman suffrage.[42]

The *Times* (Washington, DC) declared the closing session "the most interesting of all." Mattie was a featured speaker and shared the podium with Martha A. B. Conine, a member of the Colorado House, and US Senators Henry M. Teller (of Colorado) and Frank

40. Bill as amended in file of Senate Bills, 1899, Utah State Archives.

41. "Address of Mrs. Alice Merrill Horne at the Funeral Services of Martha Hughes Cannon, July 14, 1932, in the Tenth Ward Chapel, Salt Lake City, Utah," typescript in my possession.

42. "Editorial Notes," *Woman's Exponent*, Mar. 1, 1898, 253.

J. Cannon (of Utah). Representative John F. Shafroth of Colorado "spoke in glowing terms of the salutary influence the granting of suffrage to women has had in the States that have already enfranchised them." Mattie, speaking of equal suffrage in Utah, said that Utah had long been misunderstood. "The story of the struggle for woman's suffrage in Utah is the story of all efforts for the advancement and betterment of humanity, and which has been told over and over ever since the advent of civilization. ... In Utah women are not downtrodden and oppressed, but they are equal to men."[43]

The Washington Post of February 20 quoted Susan B. Anthony commenting on Senator Teller of Colorado: "Look at him! He looks a thousand times grander than a man who has not voted for women suffrage." According to Mattie, the strongest argument in favor of suffrage was that the woman voter "would not be bound by partisanship ... but will vote for the man because he is a good man. Men have to talk it over to find out what is right; but woman stays at home and rocks the cradle, and God tells her what is right."[44]

Mattie was also present, along with fifty or sixty other women, at the hearings given by the Senate Select Committee on Woman Suffrage in the Marble Room of the US Capitol. The hearings had two purposes: in the House, speakers confined their remarks to a statement of facts regarding the movement for the enfranchisement of women; in the Senate, the speeches related to the philosophy of woman's rights. Teller said: "It has been my pleasure and duty to vote against depriving women of the right of that suffrage which has been so satisfactory and successful wherever it has been tried. ... Women haven't had the opportunity to study the science of government, but if they have to vote they will study it. They are not as partisan as men because they have more conscience than men. ... I predict that in ten years there will be twice as many States where women will have the right to vote. In my judgment the movement is one of the reforms of the century, and it has come to stay and spread."

In her speech, Mattie said: "No nation can exist half free and half enslaved, and no nation can live forty-one-forty-fifths enslaved

---

43. "Women Lawmakers Speak," *Times* (Washington, DC), Feb. 20, 1898.
44. "Mason on Their Side," *Washington Post,* Feb. 20, 1898. The article includes five addresses by women, four by men.

and four-forty-fifths free. Ten years before I was old enough to vote my mother was a voter. I learned from her to vote according to conscience and not according to the dictates of political bosses. Women would not be bound by mere partisanship. If the world becomes better and liberty redeemed, it will be through the exercise of the conscience of voters on lawmakers. During the fifteen years that women have voted in Utah there has not been a defalcation in public office." Mattie also "hoped that the republic would have pure government and spread the light of truth throughout the world [which] would be more fully realized if the men of the nation allowed the women to vote with them. If women could watch over and care for the children, they could certainly express a conviction at the ballot-box, and especially so when men learn wisdom from their mother's knee."

Mattie refuted several of the fears and dire predictions of what could happen were women to receive the vote: "None of the unpleasant results which were predicted have occurred. The contentions in families, the tarnishment of woman's charm, the destruction of ideals, have all been found to be but the ghosts of unfounded prejudices. ... Women have quietly assumed the added power which always was theirs by right, and with the grace and ready adaptation to circumstances peculiar to the women of America, they have so conducted themselves that they have gained admiration and respect while losing none of their old-time prestige."[45]

Afterwards everyone attended a reception at the White House, where President William McKinley was present. Mattie wrote to Emmeline: "The most noted reception of the week was tendered by President McKinley at the White House. ... As I shook hands with him and looked into his noble face, I felt him to be a great man, notwithstanding he is not a Democrat." In the letter, Mattie was enthusiastic about the welcome "accorded her and Utah through her" and praised the work done by the convention.[46]

If Mattie had not irritated Angus enough by running for senator,

---

45. "Woman Suffrage in Utah," speech by Martha Hughes Cannon at the hearing (Feb. 15, 1898) on House Joint Resolution 68, at https://www.loc.gov.

46. "Woman's Convention. Interesting Letter from State Senator Mattie H. Cannon," *Deseret News*, Mar. 4, 1898.

they were about to go head-to-head over something that nearly ended their marriage.

Until the ratification of the Seventeenth Amendment to the Constitution in 1913, US senators were chosen by their state senators. Mattie voted twice for a US senator—once in 1897 and again in 1899.

The choice in 1897 was complicated by the consideration of former LDS Church apostle Moses Thatcher for senator. In 1895 the church had issued "The Political Rule of the Church," also known as "the political manifesto." This new policy required general authorities to get approval from the First Presidency before running for office. Thatcher was the only apostle who did not sign the document. Consequently, he was dropped from the Quorum of the Twelve in April 1896 for not being in harmony with the others, although he was not excommunicated. Angus, who assumed Mattie would also align herself with the church, opposed Thatcher's election. At first, Mattie stayed loyal to Democratic Party interests and voted for Aquila Nebeker (the senate president) and then for a Democratic attorney, Orlando W. Powers. But suddenly, on the forty-third ballot, she cast her vote for Thatcher.[47] She explained that she was afraid that if the senate remained deadlocked, a dark horse candidate, possibly a Republican, might come forward and be elected."[48] Mattie's decision no doubt incensed Angus, who placed his duty to the church over all else and would not have been able to imagine that his wife did not also.

The national and local press latched on to the unexpected move. The *Daily Capital Journal* (Salem, Oregon) related the story as welcome proof that Mormon women, when elected, would not automatically align their votes with the church's wishes.[49] The *Salt Lake Tribune* of February 2, 1897, featured a large drawing of Mattie with an accompanying article: "Senator Cannon prefaced her vote [for Thatcher] with an address so eloquent that despite parliamentary decorum and the rigid rules against demonstrations she was cheered and cheered again at its conclusion."[50] Both the speech and Mattie's

47. White, "Gentle Persuaders," 47, and "Cheered Mrs. Cannon. Paid an Eloquent Tribute to Thatcher," *Salt Lake Tribune*, Feb. 2, 1899.

48. "Cheered Mrs. Cannon. Paid an Eloquent Tribute to Thatcher."

49. "Woman's Independence," *Capital Journal* (Salem, OR), Mar. 2, 1897.

50. "Cheered Mrs. Cannon. Paid an Eloquent Tribute to Thatcher."

support for Thatcher were in vain, however.[51] In the fifty-third, and final, ballot, Joseph L. Rawlins was elected.

The 1899 senatorial election was even more difficult. Angus's son, George M. Cannon predicted the coming trouble: "The senatorial fight in the coming legislature promises to be a hot one."[52] Certainly George M. knew that sparks would fly in the legislature, but he might have been just as sure that sparks would fly between his Democratic aunt and her Republican husband. Possibly because Mattie was re-nowned for not deviating from the Democratic Party platform, she was interviewed by the chair of the Republican National Commit-tee concerning the election. The chair tried to woo her with the idea of "co-operation," which cooperation—in his opinion—would result in Frank J. Cannon, a nephew of Angus and a Republican, being re-elected.[53] Frank, who had been elected in 1896, was worried about his chances since the state legislature was overwhelmingly Demo-cratic. So, he lobbied his aunt. Mattie refused, reasoning that since she was elected a Democrat, she could not vote for a Republican. Frank left her home by the back door.[54] Angus, incensed, reportedly declared, "She will never go into another legislature and defy me again!"[55]

But 1899 also had a big surprise for Mattie. Senator David H. Peery, from Ogden, Utah, cast "the first vote ever cast for a woman for the US senate."[56] As he did, he stated: "She [Mattie] has served as a member of our state senate for two years with credit and de-serves and is entitled to the promotion."[57]

That single vote made national headlines. The *Chicago Daily Tri-bune* reported that there was no chance of her election "unless she comes in a dark horse, and her friends are now telling of such a

51. Ibid.

52. George M. Cannon, Diary, Nov. 25, 1898, George M. Cannon Journals, MS 14651, Church History Library, Church of Jesus Christ of Latter-day Saints, Salt Lake City.

53. "What Fusion Means," *Salt Lake Herald*, Mar. 15, 1898.

54. In White, "Gentle Persuaders," 48.

55. McCrimmon, untitled manuscript, 7.

56. "King Leads," *Anaconda (MO) Standard*, Jan. 20, 1899. Senator David H. Peery Jr. was, according to Elizabeth, a "rich playboy" from Ogden who often sent Mattie flow-ers. Elizabeth writes that Mattie cried when he died "soon after" (in 1901). Elizabeth Cannon Porter to Claire Noall, Feb. 13, 1938.

57. [No Title], *Beaver (OK) Herald*, Feb. 9, 1899.

possibility, owing to the present deadlock."[58] George M. Cannon, who observed the voting process, wrote that on March 9, 1899, he remained at the legislature until 12:03 a.m., "at which time the fact became apparent that no one would be elected."[59] Indeed, after 121 ballots, the senate could not elect a senator and the seat remained vacant until January 1901.

However, if Mattie had been elected, as the *St. Paul Globe* put it, "With [B. H.] Roberts in the House and Mrs. Cannon in the Senate, the American congress can look forward to its representatives from Hawaii and the Philippines with equanimity."[60] There was nothing like having a polygamist and a plural wife in Congress to pave the way for having "foreigners" become members of Congress as well!

Mattie's private life during the years 1896–99 was as complicated as her political life. Except when they saw each other in person, most of Mattie's and Angus' interaction was in the form of hastily scribbled notes from Mattie delivered by Elizabeth. Angus, however, seldom wrote notes; if he needed to talk to his wife or respond to her requests, he simply went to her house. Much of the burden of maintaining the family fell on Mattie's daughter Elizabeth, aged eleven to fourteen during that period. Mattie's great-granddaughter Joanne Peterson said that Elizabeth took care of both her brother James and Mattie, and as a result grew up fast. "She was never a child."[61]

When asked about her private life in interviews, Mattie did not hesitate to slant the truth. When Annie Laurie asked about Angus's reaction when Mattie won, she said: "I heard a prominent politician say that he wished Mr. Cannon and I had both been elected. He said he'd like to have seen the fight. He would have been disappointed. If a woman quarrels over politics with her husband, she'd quarrel with him over whether he liked biscuit or raised bread or any other subject that came to hand." All of which gives the impression that she and Angus were on the best of terms. But her marriage during her senate years was as fractious as ever.[62]

58. "Woman for Senator," *Chicago Daily Tribune*, Jan. 21, 1899.

59. George M. Cannon, Journal, Mar. 9, 1899.

60. "First Ever Cast," *St. Paul Globe*, Jan. 22, 1899. For a more cynical account, see "Our Picayunes," *Times-Picayune* (New Orleans, LA), Dec. 18, 1899.

61. JoAnn Peterson, telephone interview with the author, Aug. 21, 1988.

62. Annie Laurie, "Our Woman Senator," *Salt Lake Herald*, Nov. 11, 1895. Blanche

Angus's journal is silent during the time he and Mattie ran for senator, but beginning in May 1897, he again began chronicling his dealings with his wife. She seemed to be totally dependent upon him for support now, even though she still had a limited medical practice. Angus detailed the many times he gave her tithing scrip (an early iteration of the LDS Church's welfare program to help members who needed support) for groceries and meat, and occasionally he gave her cash, usually in response to notes she sent via Elizabeth.

Mattie's tenure as senator marked a charmed time in her life. Her star was rising, she was popular among and respected by her fellow legislators. It seemed that even the United States Senate might be within her grasp. But then something happened that would effectively end her political life.

Rose writes that "it is said" Angus never forgave Mattie her audacity in running against and defeating him in the election and that it caused a rift that was never healed (Blanche Rose, "Early Utah Medical Practice," *Utah Historical Quarterly* 10 [1942]: 20). I find no other evidence of such a rift. Certainly, there were hurt feelings and even anger and humiliation on his part in the moment. But the family maintains that their third child, Gwendolyn, was a gift of love they gave each other. So, one must conclude that if there was a rift, it was healed.

CHAPTER NINE

IMPLOSION!

Mattie was pregnant.

Throughout her life, she had proven herself to be an intelligent, courageous, if often impetuous woman. Her intelligence carried her through medical studies, and her courage enabled her to compete with men in a medical career that, while not rare for women by her time, was nonetheless difficult to accomplish. She braved the rigors of a medical education, not at a women's college, but as one of the few women in early co-educational university medical programs. She returned to Salt Lake City in a blaze of glory and high expectations. She bravely put her faith first when she became a plural wife, not knowing what to expect given the heightened anti-polygamy persecutions in the late-1800s. Although she embraced her self-chosen exile in England enthusiastically at first, the realities of being so far from home, having to obscure her identity, and being unable to practice medicine ended up being detrimental to her physical and emotional health and ultimately prevented her from resuming her medical practice with the same energy as before. Even after the birth of a second child and the difficulty of a second exile, Mattie remained optimistic and was enterprising enough to reinvent herself as a champion of women's rights and eventually to make history as the first woman state senator. So far, she had weathered all storms. She probably expected a similar storm surrounding, and another fairly favorable resolution of, her third pregnancy. But this time, things did not end as happily.

Assuming all would be well (or ignoring the possible consequences of being pregnant after the 1890 Manifesto), she did not try to hide her pregnancy but continued to live life as usual. Angus kept busy with his duties as stake president while caring for his ever-growing family. Elizabeth, age thirteen in 1898, attended school, put on plays in the front room of their home, and continued to be courier for communications between Mattie and Angus.[1] Eight-year-old James attended school and showed a growing interest in machines and electricity. He was a bit of a problem child, often skipping school and causing Mattie to despair.

Besides coping with the children, their education, and domestic disasters, Mattie continued with her political responsibilities. By the time the third legislature convened, she was visibly pregnant. Sometimes she was absent from roll-call votes during the long balloting for US senator but generally seemed to have been present to pursue her interests. Senate President Aquila Nebeker appointed her a member of several committees: Apportionment, Public Institutions, Railroads, Ways and Means, Judiciary, Labor, Education, and the Public Health Committee, of which she was named chair.[2]

In the days leading up to the birth, Angus was attentive. He visited Mattie on Sunday, April 9, 1899, and again the next Tuesday when Mattie asked him to take her for a ride that night. He regretted that he could not, as he had another engagement. He offered to have his son Quayle take her but noted resignedly in his journal that that solution gave her "no satisfaction." After dining at Sarah's house, he visited Mattie again the same evening "and the old scene is renewed. She weeps and is unhappy and I again leave her."[3]

On the following Monday (April 17), only three weeks since the legislative session had ended, Elizabeth sent word that Mattie needed Angus. "I went and found her in labor." She had asked for a nurse, but after having no luck getting one Angus called for Dr. Bascomb "only to find he was already on his way." Content that his wife

1. Elizabeth Cannon Porter to Claire Noall, Feb. 13, 1938, Special Collections, J. Willard Marriott Library, University of Utah, Salt Lake City.

2. Jean Bickmore White, "Gentle Persuaders: Utah's First Women Legislators," *Utah Historical Quarterly* 38, no. 1 (Winter 1970): 47. See also Shari Siebers Crall, "'Something More': A Biography of Martha Hughes Cannon," (honors thesis, Brigham Young University, 1985), 87.

3. Angus M. Cannon, Diary, Apr. 9 and 11, April 1899, MS 1200, Church History Library, Church of Jesus Christ of Latter-day Saints, Salt Lake City, Utah.

was in good hands, Angus went to breakfast. When he returned, the doctor told him he had wanted her to go to the hospital to give birth, but that now there was no time. "It was about 12 pm when a little girl was born. The Dr. said things are as well as you can expect." That afternoon, Elizabeth contacted him with a list of things Mattie wanted. In the evening Angus went to her and "found her getting along very well."[4]

It did not take long for the local press to get wind of the child's birth. On April 20 a friend called on Angus to let him know a *Tribune* reporter had been sniffing around and wanted to know the sex of the child. Angus called on Mattie later the same morning when the *Tribune* reporter caught up with him and, upon hearing a child cry, wanted the nurse to tell him about it. The nurse replied that "the cry of a child did not indicate its parentage." Despite their attempt at subterfuge, the next morning Angus read the headlines in the *Tribune*: "President Angus and Senator Mattie Hughes Cannon had born to them last Saturday a girl."[5]

Mattie was worn out; the baby cried much of the time, Elizabeth was sick, and James refused to go to school. To make matters worse, when Mattie tried to order groceries, her scrip was discounted. She and Angus were both distraught. He visited her, administered to her, and "left her weeping."[6]

On April 25, Angus again visited Mattie and blessed their daughter, giving her the name Gwendolyn. Though local reporters were starting to get wind of Gwendolyn in April, it was not until July that the scandal hit the national and international press. The headlines were sensational, all noting with outrage that LDS Church members in Utah had apparently not honored their promise to discontinue plural marriage. Typical headlines were: "Mormon Arrested," "Lived with a Plural Wife," and "The Baby of Two Statesmen."[7] *The Idaho Statesman* was indignant: "The people of the entire country are aroused over the polygamous practices of these Mormon leaders,

4. Angus M. Cannon, Diary, Apr. 17, 1899.

5. Angus M. Cannon, Diary, Apr. 20, 1899.

6. Angus M. Cannon, Diary, Apr. 21, 1899.

7. "Mormon Arrested," *Iowa State Bystander*, July 14, 1899; "Lived with a Plural Wife," *Kansas City Star*, July 9, 1899; and "The Baby of Two Statesmen," *Wichita Daily Eagle*, July 21, 1899.

and they have determined to strike at the head of the hideous monster of plural marriage whenever it shall present itself."[8]

The *San Francisco Chronicle Special Dispatch* of July 9, 1899, noted that "[The Cannons'] political differences" apparently did not "mar their friendly relations."[9]

Gradually more facts were revealed. "A warrant, based upon a complaint sworn to by the representative of a New York newspaper, was issued today from the County Attorney's office for the arrest of Pres. Angus M, Cannon of the Salt Lake Stake of the Mormon church, charging him with polygamy, which is cited as being contrary to [Utah law]." Angus's attorney son, John M. Cannon, "appeared before a justice of the peace and accepted service on behalf of his father and also filed bond of $300 for his father's appearance on Friday next."[10]

"No one questions for a moment that Cannon is guilty," said one newspaper. "He does not deny it, but he is not discussing the matter now, though at the time of the birth of Mrs. Cannon's last child in April he is said to have accepted the customary congratulations with his usual grace."[11]

Angus was not as unaffected as that article implied. Another reporter noted that Angus, seen at the Tithing Office, "was perspiring freely and looked sorely troubled, but firmly declined to discuss the matter in any of its phases." Mattie seemed to be holding up to the scrutiny better. When visited at home,

> Mrs. Cannon was attired in a rose-colored tea gown, trimmed in cream lace, and appeared to be enjoying the best of health. When told the mission of that reporter, she seemed not a bit disturbed, and calmly but decidedly replied that she had nothing to say for publication. Her manner was extremely gracious, but it could easily be seen that she was not to be swerved from her decision in the matter. Mrs. Cannon objects to newspaper notoriety, and intimated that she had received more than her share of late. After replying that she did not wish to make a statement

---

8. "Angus M. Cannon Arrested," *Idaho Statesman*, July 10, 1899.

9. "If a Jury Can Be Found to Convict the Salt Lake Leader Wholesale Prosecutions May Be Made," *San Francisco Chronicle Special Dispatch*, July 9, 1899.

10. "Angus M. Cannon Arrested," *Idaho Statesman*, July 9, 1899.

11. "If a Jury Can Be Found." Also, "Lived with a Plural Wife," which reads, "It is believed he will plead guilty and pay a fine."

for publication, Mrs. Cannon put the question aside and did not refer to it again, although she chatted pleasantly for some little time on various other topics of general interest.[12]

The *Salt Lake Herald* reported that Mattie responded, probably alluding to her once more being in the press when her husband was charged with polygamy: "I do not know what will be done, and I cannot say anything except that I hope the matter will now be settled for all time." And she "delightedly" showed off ten-week-old Gwendolyn, who was the cause of "all the rumpus."[13]

It was assumed in advance that the punishment would be too lenient. Most accounts concluded that Angus would be fined around $300 and/or receive a jail sentence of not more than six months. "Senator Martha Hughes Cannon, mother-like, says she must not worry over the result of the case, because she has to get strong and well to take her baby away from the hot weather and the city."[14] The *St. Louis Post–Dispatch* reported gleefully what most observers hoped: "Mormon Cannon Pleads Guilty to Polygamy and Will Suffer."[15]

In the end, the national press was disappointed that neither Angus nor Mattie suffered legally in any way. The *Saint Paul Globe* reported the results of the case in staccato headlines: "Easy for Mr. Cannon. The Utah Mormon With Four Wives Smiles at a $100 Fine. His Trial a Big Farce. The Offenders Openly Admit Their Guilt of a Plural Marriage—A Baby Girl in the Case." The article went on to state that LDS leaders were "brazenly champion[ing] polygamy. No attempt at concealment is made."[16]

Although most newspapers only described Mattie as the mother of the child without assigning her any guilt, the *Denver Evening Post* came closest to casting blame on her, pointing out the irony of her being a senator who made the laws, yet broke them herself, writing that she was the "most prominent woman in the emancipated

---

12. "Caused a Sensation," *Helena Independent*, July 13, 1899.

13. "Exhibited the Baby," *Salt Lake Herald*, July 9, 1899.

14. "The Baby of Two Statesman," *Wichita Daily Eagle*, July 21, 1899.

15. "Mormon Cannon Pleads Guilty to Polygamy and Will Suffer," *St. Louis Post-Dispatch*, July 23, 1899.

16. "Easy for Mr. Cannon. The Utah Mormon with Four Wives Smiles at a $100 Fine. His Trial a Big Farce. The Offenders Openly Admit Their Guilt of a Plural Marriage—A Baby Girl in the Case," *Saint Paul Globe*, Aug. 6, 1899.

community. She has served the state law-making body for two terms and all the time has been 'living h￾ r religion.'"[17]

The scandal reopened old fears and suspicions that all was not well in Utah despite the Manifesto that forbade polygamous marriages. The wider public had interpreted the Manifesto to mean that the church would not only not perform further polygamous marriages but would abandon any existing polygamous relationships. Many men who had plural wives did not see it that way. In his journal, Angus made his stance clear: "The Manifesto only prohibited us from taking more wives, at that time … [but] no man has authority to dissolve the obligations my wives and I have taken upon us, with[out] our consent. Under these circumstances, I am prepared to acknowledge Martha Hughes Cannon is my wife and that little Gwendolyn is our daughter.[18]

Mattie's political career was essentially over. There was no more talk of her being considered as a US senator. She never ran for political office again.

Having a newborn, along with two older children, at age forty-one was not easy for Mattie. She struggled with her health, with the patience needed to tend a newborn, with finding good hired help, and—as usual—with finances. Angus recorded many of these ups and downs in his journal. His entry on April 28, 1899, is typical: "I find Martha very poorly and out of patience with her hired girl and the nurse. The former was gone all yesterday afternoon and then at night permitted girls to talk with her outside the house while the nurse entertained her sweetheart inside, making Martha very nervous and sick. To add to her discomfort the babe cried and compelled her to sit up with it to her great injury. I left her weeping and feeling very bad."[19]

Interspersed with accounts of his church duties and activities with his other families, Angus—always in despair that he could not always provide his family members with what they wanted—kept records of what he spent. Through June, for example, he records

17. "Another Political Scandal in Utah," *Denver Evening Post*, Apr. 21, 1899.
18. Angus M. Cannon, Diary, July 12, 1899.
19. Angus M. Cannon, Diary, Apr. 28, 1899.

buying a shawl for Gwendolyn and giving Mattie tithing orders and money to pay her hired girl and back wages for the nurse.[20]

Acerbic as ever, Mattie sent Angus a note via Elizabeth in November 1899 telling him she had new household help, who "does considerable housework while I attend 'Gwennie' who demands considerable attention." However, she made sure that Angus knew she was not happy with having to do so much of the housework and cooking herself: "[I] revel in rag patching and every minute is thus employed and all so delicious and so interesting to write to my husband."[21] During the next six months Mattie and Angus's personal life went from problematic, because of finances, to terrible when Mattie threatened to leave him. Angus tried, but his available time and money just was not enough to appease his wife.

A month later, in October 1899, Mattie's home was threatened with foreclosure, and she still needed to buy clothing for the children. Angus had sent her some money in response to a note in which she complained of having to sew rags "for your children" and asked him to grant her a final interview before she filed for divorce and left town.[22]

The next day, Sunday, Angus visited her and recorded that evening: "She complained as I left that I always had engagements to take me away again when I called upon her. I on the other hand wondered she should desire my company when she desired to be divorced from me."[23]

Mattie continually lashed out at Angus, blaming him for her situation. She had broken down crying in the company of the mission president and elders in Birmingham, and followed that scene with a scathing letter to Angus accusing him of never loving her or trying to understand and meet her needs. That she had contributed to her current situation by pursuing her political ambitions, neglecting her medical practice, and requiring expensive clothes and household help did not seem to occur to her. The combination of a difficult recovery from childbirth and disappointment about the ending of

20. Angus M. Cannon, Diary, May 25, 26, 27, Jun. 12, 24, 1899.
21. Martha Hughes Cannon to Angus M. Cannon, Nov. 1899, Angus M. Cannon Papers, MS 1200, Church History Library.
22. Angus M. Cannon, Diary, Nov. 11, 1899.
23. Angus M. Cannon, Diary, Nov. 12, 1899.

her political career heightened the intensity of her emotions. In her distress, she latched on to the one threat that would wound her husband the most. It is unlikely that she ever intended to pursue a divorce, but her threat remained a sore point with him. Interestingly, although her relationship with Angus remained volatile, there was no mention of divorce after this.

There is no record of Mattie actively maintaining a medical practice after Gwendolyn's birth.[24] In fact, Angus wrote in his journal (amid detailing one of their quarrels over money) that he had told her: "You make no use of your profession to [supply] your necessities while I exert every power of which I am possessed to supply [them]."[25]

However, Mattie did continue in her role as physician for Angus and members of his family. In mid-December Angus visited her complaining of leg pain. She advised him to use tincture of arnica, rest it, and not to walk on it until it was better. A few days later, he was back because he could hardly hobble around. Mattie told him: "When I said to you last Tuesday you should keep off your leg until it is better, I did not expect you to regard what I said, but now I see you will do as I say—because you cannot get about on it." She continued to prescribe that he wrap it with arnica fermented with wild sage until it was better. But the next day, when he called again, she changed the treatment to hot linseed oil, saying it was more healing.[26]

Although she never held political office again, over the next two decades Mattie remained active in political and civic affairs and continued to be a sought-after speaker. She was, for example, a delegate at the Democratic state convention in 1901, and in 1902 was appointed vice president of the American Congress of Tuberculosis in Utah.[27]

24. Both Shari Crall and Keith Terry write that Martha returned to practicing medicine following the third legislature, became an authority on narcotic addiction, and did a special study on nervous diseases. Shari Siebers Crall, "'Something More': A Biography of Martha Hughes Cannon," (honors thesis, Brigham Young University, 1985), and Keith Calvin Terry, "The Contribution of Medical Women During the First Fifty Years in Utah," (master's thesis, Brigham Young University, 1964), 51. This may be true, but I can find no evidence of it beyond familial anecdotes.

25. Angus M. Cannon, Diary, Sept. 25, 1903.

26. Angus M. Cannon, Diary, Dec. 19, 23, and 24, 1899.

27. "American Congress of Tuberculosis," *The Sanitarian* 48 (Apr. 1, 1902).

The *Salt Lake Telegram* reported that Mattie spoke to a group at the Lagoon amusement park, north of Salt Lake City, to honor Senator J. L. Rawlins in June 1902.[28] The next year she was again on the shores of the Great Salt Lake, but at the Saltair resort, accompanying Charles W. Penrose and several women, all of whom had been plural wives. The occasion was the visit of Ella Wheeler Wilcox, a world-famous writer and poet, who was in Salt Lake City to find out about polygamy—as it was, and as it had become. In her book *The Worlds and I* Wilcox writes: "Important events in one's life often become dim in memory, while lesser incidents stand forth clearly. A day in Salt Lake City, Utah, I have never forgotten, where I went out to see the remains of the Salt Sea, in company with twenty-two women who had all been polygamous wives."

Despite categorizing her visit as a "lesser incident," Wilcox was impressed with Penrose's eloquence as he explained why polygamous wives were happier than single wives and why their children were mentally and physically superior to non-Mormon children. Reading the words Wilcox attributed to Penrose, one clearly hears Mattie's views on motherhood and the rearing of children. He and Mattie were good friends; he must have consulted with her as he composed his speech. But all his powers of articulation could not convince Ella Wilcox. She countered: "I assured the Elder I believed men in general had much to learn from the Mormons regarding the right view of fatherhood, and the obligation to protect and care for the expectant mother, but I could not regard the polygamous wife with any feeling, save one of pity. 'I would rather,' I said, 'be a deceived wife, or the unfortunate affinity even, on whom the world looks askance than accept the position of one of a syndicate owning stock in a husband.'" The photograph taken on that day has the entire party posing on the large outdoor staircase leading up to the main entrance of Saltair. Wilcox counted twenty-two women; the photograph depicts seventeen women, one child, and Penrose. Several prominent women were there: Emmeline B. Wells, Romania Pratt Penrose, and Mattie.[29]

---

28. "Democrats at Lagoon," *Salt Lake Telegram*, Jun. 17, 1902.

29. Ella Wheeler Wilcox, *The Worlds and I* (New York: George H. Doran Co., 1918), 300–15. This quotation is on p. 311.

In Mattie's post-Gwendolyn political life, it is clear that she never wavered in her allegiance to the Democratic Party. In 1906 she was a featured speaker at the Woman's Democratic Club in Salt Lake City where she gave an address in memory of Thomas Jefferson.[30] Ten years later, in 1916, the *Salt Lake Telegram* humorously reported her travels to speak for Democratic candidates: "Dr. Cannon Speaks at 13 Rallies; She's Not Superstitious." And "she has addressed 13 Democratic rallies and will have traveled 1300 miles by the time she arrives in Salt Lake City."[31]

By 1904, she was already living part-time in Los Angeles where her son, James, now age sixteen, had gone to live. At least one California community was thrilled to know that the first female state senator was living in their state. The paper reported: "Dr. Martha Hughes Cannon, a state senator of Utah, has gone to live in California with the intention of helping the women of that state to get equal suffrage. She is described as a powerful and witty speaker."[32] However, there is no record of her participating in any suffrage activities on behalf of California women. Her focus in life was now her children and grandchildren.

In the period leading up to Angus's death in 1915, his and Mattie's relationship maintained a predictable pattern: a day of good relations followed by days of difficulties. James, and to a lesser degree Elizabeth, were often unwittingly the cause of their fights, which were escalating in both tone and action.

Some of their arguments seem trivial, such as Angus's objection to Mattie subscribing to the *Salt Lake Herald* (which he referred to as a "disreputable sheet")[33] instead of the *Deseret News*, but this was a continuing and ever-deepening dispute. Angus seemed to think it proved she was not as faithful to the church as she should be. At one point, as they argued, Angus exploded, "I know you don't care a damn for me and I do not for you! You care nothing for me except when you want something."[34]

30. "Jefferson's Memory Will Be Honored," *Salt Lake Telegram*, Apr. 13, 1906.
31. "Dr. Cannon Speaks at 13 Rallies; She's Not Superstitious," *Salt Lake Telegram*, Nov. 5, 1916.
32. "To Help Cause in Pacific State," *Hobart (OK) Daily Republican*, Nov. 11, 1908.
33. Angus M. Cannon, Diary, Feb. 7, 1902.
34. Angus M. Cannon, Diary, June 1901.

Mattie still did not file for divorce, and the marital battles continued. About three months later, at the beginning of September 1904, Angus recorded that they had had several "plain talks" which disturbed him enough that he could not sleep. He yelled; she wept. Finally, on September 9, she told him that she was leaving with the children the next morning and going to California for six weeks, where she planned to enroll Elizabeth at Stanford University and put James in high school. Her health was the main excuse for this trip, as she (clearly in menopause) wrote to Angus later: "These night sweats that had come upon me were making such progress in the way of weakening my system—and nothing I did seemed to check them at all, only temporarily, that it would not have been long before I would have been down and had to be waited upon. But I feel that this trip is going to put me all right again."[35] She asked for his "good feelings" and promised to bring the children to his office the next morning to say goodbye. Angus wrote: "I feel strange on account of this conduct which is in keeping with her whole life as my wife. I have told her, 'Martha, you have been a law unto yourself always since you have been my wife.'" He waited for them the next day in vain. She and the children left without seeing him. Angus, uncharacteristically, took to his bed until well into the afternoon of the next day.[36]

Mattie half-apologized for her behavior but tempered it with a warning not to block her desires: "Don't worry about our little misunderstandings—Yours and mine—with temperaments and dispositions so radical, and so much alike, I think we have done marvelously well in our 20 years of married life. Please do not try, dearest, to hedge up my way whatsoever; life is hard enough without that." Mattie hoped she would be able to relocate permanently to Pacific Grove, a coastal community in Monterey, California, which she considered essential to her health.

Mattie and the children were back in Salt Lake City on January 3, 1905. But the time apart had not improved Mattie's and Angus's relationship. On February 5, he told her that he would not "call on her to receive her abuse in the future and she might complain of

35. Martha Hughes Cannon to Angus M. Cannon, Sep. 11, 1904.
36. Angus M. Cannon, Diary, Sep. 5–10, 1904.

me and have me brought before the teachers or Bishop of the ward. She had said in the presence of my children she would complain of me to the President of the Church and I supposed she had done so, [denouncing] my 'influence in the Priesthood and [that I] delighted in imposing on a little woman.'"

She had gone to church president Joseph F. Smith to complain—Charles W. Penrose reported to Angus that he had seen Mattie coming out of his office. Angus recorded that he spoke with Smith himself, who said, "Angus, what is the matter with Mattie? You had better look out for her." Angus asked, "Has she seen you and complained? She threatened months since to do so and I said: 'I shall be only too glad to have him hear you!'"[37]

A year later, on January 26, 1906, Angus called on Mattie and was floored by her newest request. She proposed selling her house and, with the $2,000 equity, build a house in Ocean Grove, California, using plans drawn up by James. She told him she needed to be at sea level for her health and could "get along all right" if he would promise to give her $35.00 a month for living expenses. He answered, "I cannot do it. I only get $1000.00 a year by the kindness of my brethren, who may withdraw it at any time. Were I to give you this amount out of $900.00, being all I have after paying my tithing, I would only have, after taking out $420.00 for you I would have but $480.00 left to support myself and four other families. I have been favored of God, who has given me my children and I shall not consent for them to be taken from the country [out of Utah], let consequences be what they may. If you have any complaint to make, do so to my bishop and let him judge between us. You have been a law to yourself and you will have to do what you do on your own back for I shall consent to nothing of the kind." Mattie burst out, "I cannot live unless I go to sea level." Angus left her still crying and later recorded, "These scenes are very distressing to me and I experience more trouble with this self-willed woman than I have had with all the rest of my family put together."[38]

What *was* wrong with Mattie? These and similar scenes ongoing from the time of Gwendolyn's birth to Angus's death in 1915 were

---

37. Angus M. Cannon, Diary, Feb. 5–6, 1905.
38. Angus M. Cannon, Diary, Jan. 26, 1906.

centered on the same themes: requests for money that Angus was either unwilling or unable to grant; Mattie's inability to control James; Mattie's mood swings—from accompanying Angus to concerts and funerals to disparaging him and his other families—which seemed to prevent any sustained dialogue between the two; Mattie's worry that she would lose her home; and Angus's worry that she would complain of his treatment of her to church headquarters and demand a divorce. Both of them were avid journal writers and recorded their meetings and contentions in vivid language. Angus's journals are extant, but they give only his side of the conflict. Mattie's journals must have been even more colorful, and apparently Angus had either read them or feared what was in them, for in the midst of an argument, he cried out, "I wish your journals were all burned!"[39] Sadly, his wish was eventually granted, and we can only guess at Mattie's motivations.

Mattie had always demonstrated a mercurial temperament, which worsened after Gwendolyn's birth, exacerbated by the loss of her political career and financial stress. Mattie's great-granddaughter said that Mattie suffered from what the family calls "Black Mariahs"—their term for the combination of depression, panic attacks, and anxiety Mattie demonstrated. It is easy to see how this could affect her rationality in times of stress, contributing to her escalating battles with Angus.

One obvious question is, "Why did she not earn money for herself?" Early in her career her medical practice made her relatively wealthy; she owned land, horses, and a fine wardrobe. However, after her exile to England, although she revived her practice several times and flirted with running a nursing school, her efforts seemed rather hit-and-miss and she never regained her financial footing. With the rise of her political career, medicine definitely took a backseat. But most importantly perhaps, she had lost confidence in herself as a physician.[40] When she graduated from medical school in 1880, she was trained in the latest methods and with the most up-to-date medical knowledge. But the intervening two decades marked a great increase in medical theory and treatment that she had not kept up with, such

---

39. Angus M. Cannon, Diary, Mar. 2, 1903.
40. JoAnn Petersen, telephone interview with the author, Aug. 21, 1988.

as the development of vaccines and the discovery of aspirin.[41] However, her senate activity proved that she was up-to-date in matters of public health. Her granddaughter remembered that she always advocated deep breathing and exercise and that, because of her medical training, she was "very caring and would recognize when people needed some help along the way."[42] As Angus's diaries indicate, Mattie continued to give medical care and advice to family members. Her granddaughter Helen Ovard remembers Mattie painlessly "mending" a gash on her face, and Elizabeth said her mother was a "keen diagnostician" and a "natural psychologist"—all talents that would stand Mattie in good stead as she returned to private life.[43]

41. For example, see www.library.duke.edu/digitalcollections/mma/timeline.

42. Nancy Green, interview with the author, 2012.

43. Helen Ovard Cannon, interview with the author, Aug. 1988; Elizabeth C. McCrimmon, "Dr. Martha Hughes Cannon; First Woman State Senator in America," unpublished manuscript, 7, Utah State Historical Society.

CHAPTER TEN

POST-POLITICAL LIFE

For the period following Gwendolyn's birth, the paper trail for Mattie Cannon is very thin. Newspaper mentions are largely confined to a few notices of her fundraising efforts and the marriages of her children. There are no notices advertising a medical practice. Her letters to Angus are sometimes informative, but most often are simply requests for money or tithing office scrip to purchase clothing for the children and household items. More illuminating are several letters from Elizabeth to her father. Contemporaries and friends of Mattie, including Emmeline B. Wells and Charles W. Penrose, made only fleeting (and sometimes cryptic) mention of her in letters or in their journals.

For two decades, Mattie's life swung back and forth between Salt Lake City and California. She remained a somewhat familiar figure—albeit more minor—in Utah public life and politics. For example, in October 1909, she gave a speech on hygiene and sanitation at the Relief Society general conference in the Salt Lake Tabernacle. Her remarks centered on the importance of preventing disease and giving young women training in hygiene and nursing.[1]

Mattie was in Pacific Grove for the fall and early winter of 1904 and 1906 as well as for a few months in 1907. Elizabeth wrote to her father on October 16, 1904, bringing him up to date: Mattie and the children were staying in Pacific Grove as guests of Mrs. Libbie Pettit for ten days, who "treated us royally." Using part of her monthly allowance from Angus, Mattie rented a "dear little house with the twinkling lights of the village in front, the great pure forest in back, and the blue bay of Monterey on the north."

---

1. "Relief Society Holds Conference," *Salt Lake Tribune*, Oct. 8, 1909.

Elizabeth was preparing to return to Salt Lake City to attend the University of Utah, but she left with "a dull, leaden ache at my heart on account of going away from my mother. She is a <u>very</u> <u>very</u> [underlined twice] <u>very</u> [underlined three times] sick woman and if it were not for her knowledge of 'bracing up' with medicines and her sublime <u>grit</u> she would be flat on her back. She had faith in this climate and will probably be benefitted if she stays here a while." Mattie had joined, according to Elizabeth, the "droves of invalids [who] are made well in the balmy atmosphere."[2]

On December 2, 1904, Mattie wrote to Angus ruefully that the doctor in Pacific Grove "says I have 'entered the period in a woman's life of gloom, phantoms, shadows and despair.' 'Change of life.'" In addition, the doctor said she was in poor physical condition and was suffering from rheumatism. Though she noted than men do not go through a similar process as they age, she also said (with some satisfaction, it seems) that, as Angus had passed his seventieth birthday, "the appearance of things must assert themselves to some extent" even for him. She hoped to stay at least two more months, as the doctor said she "must not return to the mountains on account of a weakness of the heart's action."[3]

By March 1905, they were all back in Salt Lake City, but in July 1906, Mattie and Gwendolyn were again established in Pacific Grove. While there, on August 3, 1906, she wrote to Angus that she and the children had been in San Francisco not long after the April 18 earthquake that nearly destroyed the city. She wrote: "Poor San Francisco, 'tis the same no more. We had to walk *everywhere*, line and lines of policemen in evidence, little traffic conveyance for go-ers about except in crowded carry-alls—necessitating *long* tiresome waits. People were alarmed to go on the few street cars running, fearing such 'infernal machines.' This was my first travelling experience for me since being sick and was rather too much for me. ... Well, I will soon be home to what purpose I know not." She was tired, ill, and discouraged. "'Tis lovely here [Pacific Grove] and beautiful and

2. Elizabeth Rachel Cannon to Angus M. Cannon, Oct. 6, 1904, Angus M. Cannon Papers, MS 1200, Church History Library, Church of Jesus Christ of Latter-day Saints, Salt Lake City.

3. Martha Hughes Cannon to Angus M. Cannon, Dec. 2, 1904, Angus M. Cannon Papers.

I dread to leave not that I am so much in love with the place ... but I fear my health; it never was worth much in Salt Lake especially since I was married and I fear it never will be [very good]. To cap the climax I am sadly in need of an operation, as things have all been wrong ever since the birth of Gwendolyn very much so but I never once since then felt I could survive a long period of chloroforming and cutting that the experts put one through now-a-days." She could not help giving Angus a dig, observing that he had not the opportunity to get to know Gwendolyn. Still, she signed the letter, "Your loving wife, Martha H. Cannon."[4]

A week later, Mattie wrote to Angus telling him about her depression and spells, which she describes as "periods of weakness or faintness, when I got so limp I can't move, but simply perspire and sweat until there appears to be no more moisture in my body." Furthermore, her feet were so swollen that she had to buy new shoes, "much larger than my number 4's." She said when she told her physician that she intended to return to Salt Lake City, he replied, "Why, doctor, you ought to know that it is the worst thing you could do, to go to a higher altitude, your only salvation lies in remaining at sea-level." She assured Angus that the cost of living in her "little cottage by the sea" was much less than it would have been had she remained in Salt Lake City and had to purchase coal, and then begged him to send her allowance as soon as possible.[5]

In a November 1906 letter, she wrote, "I am so miserable, I cannot do anything but grunt & complain from morning until night, about my miseries and restless and sleepless at night; I hardly believed someone could get into such forlorn condition and retain their senses—from day to day. I wonder what I have done to merit such punishment." And then she immediately answered her own question.

> I attempted to hold up too long, and do too much while educating the children, I should have given up sooner and sought help earlier. As it was, I kept on and on! Taking stimulants of various kinds, to keep up on until now, and for several years, my poor heart will not beat at all at all, without artificial pumping pumping—I know now, I would not have lived a month in the high altitude, the way I was running

---

4. Martha Hughes Cannon to Angus M. Cannon, Aug. 3, 1907.
5. Martha Hughes Cannon to Angus M. Cannon, Oct. 16, 1906.

down before I left, as the heart-tonic pills I was taking, then without which, the heart apparently, would not beat at all, at all, would no longer stay on my stomach. That was why I was so miserable as you saw me, in the morning, the effects of the heart-stimulants taken before retiring, had worn off, in the morning and that taken in the morning, could scarcely, towards the last few weeks before I left, be retained on the stomach, so I had to pump the ingredients—nitroglycerine, strophanthin, strychnia-atropine, etc.—into the rectum. Altogether I am a miserable <u>wreck</u>.[6]

While writing, she was (as she would say) growing morbid, hoping only that she could live long enough to see "Elizabeth and James with their respective partners in life … kneel at the marriage altar in the Temple of Our God—and settled honorably. … When this is accomplished, I know that Gwendolyn will be well taken care of, for both James and Elizabeth dearly love '*Little Mikey-Ann*' as they term her."[7]

After reading Mattie's letters dealing with her health, Samuel M. Brown, MD, believes that Mattie suffered from congestive heart failure—the cause of her swollen legs and heart palpitations—making it difficult for her to climb stairs and leaving her prone to breathlessness, even while lying flat. She had probably become dependent on the low doses of strychnine.

All of it was complicated by her self-prescribed, often ineffective treatments—all with undesirable side effects. The drugs she was taking went from giving her a slight pick-me-up (concoctions of strychnine) to having no effect at all (atropine). He finds her to have been a woman with great courage to have nonetheless pushed through all that.

Brown also comments on her mental health, saying that she had a well-established pattern of overworking herself. As a physician, she would have recognized the symptoms of mental illness (depression and anxiety) and the accompanying physical problems in herself because "the belief that emotional stress, fear, anxiety, dread

6. Strophanthin is a poisonous substance of the glycoside class, used at the time as a heart stimulant.
7. Martha Hughes Cannon to Angus M. Cannon, Nov. 18 and 20, 1906.

and depression could cause you to have physical illness was very established in her day"—yet she overcame it. "She would have been embarrassed to admit just how sad and anxious and troubled she was feeling" because mental illness carried a stigma with it then, as it does now. Brown is of the opinion that "she took some of that nervous energy and anguish that came from depression and anxiety and made a real difference."

Perhaps Mattie was able to work through much of that despair and anguish by writing crazed letters to Angus. Beginning during her English exile and continuing up to Angus's death, she engaged in a sort of stream-of-consciousness writing, emptying her emotions into letters, perhaps so that she could remain rational and controlled during her interactions with others.

Brown sums Mattie up as a woman "racked with self-doubt about her weakness—Why can't I always be happy? Why am I anxious? Why do I need medications to function? And you can imagine there would have been a dialogue for her internally about who she is and what she's worth. It's sad that somebody so successful and capable and giving would have been beset by those kinds of doubts. But I think it's probably more common than we realize that people who are driven are not just driven, but a little haunted."[8]

Even though Mattie was pragmatic, generally accepting life as it unfolded, it must have been deflating, at best, to be on the pinnacle of political success one moment, and vilified, with no political future, the next. Her anxiety certainly stemmed, in part, from overwork and impossible expectations (from herself and from others).

Elizabeth married Roy Porter on July 17, 1912, in the Salt Lake Temple and celebrated with the family at a wedding breakfast hosted by Elizabeth's half-sister, Ann Cannon, at Angus's home in Forest Dale (Salt Lake City). It was a joyful occasion for Mattie and Angus, but it was overshadowed by the death of Angus's wife Sarah Maria Mousley on March 12, leaving Angus with four living wives.

A few months before Elizabeth and Roy married, Mattie had

---

8. Brown, quoted in an interview with Nancy Green for the KUED documentary *Martha Hughes Cannon,* July 2012. Brown teaches pulmonary and critical care medicine, medical ethics, and humanities at the Intermountain Medical Center at the University of Utah, Salt Lake City, Utah.

another health crisis. She had gone to New York City to have her neuritis treated. Alarming reports about her condition reached Elizabeth, who rushed to New York to bring her mother home. She wrote Angus:

> Found mother at the hospital here and must confess, in much better condition than I expected to find her. So wrought up was I from the reports that I half expected to take her home in a box. She is still weak, but we have been getting her out every day and she has been slowly improving. She had sat alone in a gloomy hotel room so long thinking how sick she was, that she had become morbid. She had had an acute attack of gastritis followed by an ulcerated sore throat, and bracing up to make the additional effort to come home, finished her and gave her a relapse. The Doctors here at the hospital are fine men (one young Welshman especially) and they have done all that they could for her and made a success of her case. The rest depends on her and her family helping her to build up. So far she has shown a grim courage such as not one woman in a thousand would have done. Tho' stories are conflicting everyone agrees that she ought to have had someone with her when she left the hospital. Of all concerned, I think mother is the least to blame ... I think [she] can weather the journey [home even though] she has had two pretty bad nights lately—one caused by exhaustion [from the] Turkish bath.[9]

Elizabeth moved with her new husband to his isolated Oasis Ranch (also known as Brighton Ranch) located at 1300 South 4400 West in the Salt Lake Valley. The Oasis Ranch was a large grazing area between the alkali flats and the agricultural belt, with 600 apple trees, one and a half acres of pear trees, and fields of alfalfa, wheat, and barley.

However, Roy died suddenly on August 8, 1919, only seven years into their marriage, of a cerebral hemorrhage brought on by chronic high blood pressure. Mattie and Gwendolyn had been fixtures at the ranch off and on for several years, but at Roy's death, Elizabeth was in such shock that Mattie and Gwendolyn moved out to help her. Elizabeth later wrote: "When my husband, Roy S. Porter, dropped dead on 15 minutes notice, Aug. 8, 1919, leaving me with an alkali ranch and 2 baby girls,—one seven weeks the other 3½ years.

---

9. Elizabeth Rachel Cannon to Angus M. Cannon, Mar. 24, 1912.

Mother came out and took care of the children and ran the ranch house (wherever she was, comfort and charm sprang up), while I sold the livestock and saved the land."[10]

Although Mattie concentrated on helping Elizabeth with the children and the ranch, she was still active politically, albeit on the fringe of events. For example, in 1916, the Salt Lake County Democrats chose her as one of the delegates to their convention, she being listed as the Brighton District delegate, which is where the Oasis Ranch was located.[11]

Mattie and Gwendolyn remained at the ranch for seven years. Elizabeth tried leasing the ranch to a cousin—unsuccessfully, as she objected to the cousin installing a moonshine still on the property. After two more years, Elizabeth finally sold the ranch, and she, Gwendolyn, and Gwendolyn's husband, Gerald Quick, made their final move to Los Angeles, traveling in a Model T Ford.[12]

Gwendolyn was the source of Mattie's fall from politics, but also her greatest joy. In a letter to Angus on November 18, 1904, Mattie wrote: "I could write chapters on this 'Ghwendo' of ours where life is one bright song of sunshine from morning until night—flowers, shells, pinecones, and oak-balls (the latter she strings by the yard for beads) are her ever delight." Elizabeth and James were equally smitten. Elizabeth wrote: "[Mother] used to sing Gwendolyn to sleep, but Gwen informed her that she didn't tell the Mowgli stories right. I had told my small sister the Kipling ones, but mother just made them up."[13]

Gwendolyn was lively, beautiful, funny, strong-willed, and stylish—a devotee of flapper clothing. She married a neighbor she met while at Elizabeth's Oasis Ranch—Lieutenant Gerald Churchill Quick—whom she had seen in his uniform and fallen in love with.[14] They eloped in 1922 to Quick's hometown, Los Angeles. The couple had one son, Jerry Jr., nicknamed "Bokie."

10. Elizabeth Cannon Porter to Claire Noall, Feb. 13, 1938, Special Collections, J. Willard Marriott Library, University of Utah, Salt Lake City; and Mary Idelia Porter Ober Nichols, "History of Elizabeth Cannon Porter McCrimmon, Compiled by Her Daughter," Jan. 1989, 17, 18, 25–27, 32, copy in my possession.

11. "County Democrats Choose Delegates to Convention," *Salt Lake Telegram,* Mar. 29, 1916, 6.

12. Nichols, "History of Elizabeth Rachel Cannon Porter McCrimmon," 24, 30.

13. Elizabeth Cannon Porter to Claire Noall, Mar. 12, 1938.

14. JoAnn Petersen, telephone interview with the author, Aug. 21, 1988.

Being so vivacious and determined to enjoy life, Gwendolyn found it difficult "to settle down and pay a lot of attention to her health." Elizabeth recorded the consequences: "Gwendolyn ... caught a bad cold after driving to Ventura in an open touring car." This later developed into pneumonia, first in one lung then the other. It left her with tuberculosis. In those days, "they didn't have the modern drugs; if you got tuberculosis, the thing you could count on mostly was good care, lots of sleep, good nutrition. She lived in a damp house over cold garages on the banks of the Arroyo Secco," which did not help. In an attempt to get her to a higher altitude, Elizabeth purchased a one-story, barn-like, unfinished house at 635 Dimmick Drive on Mt. Washington. "We had it finished, and she came up and played the mandolin for us the next Thanksgiving." Then Gerald came home with influenza, which he passed on to his wife. Too late, Gwendolyn had finally consented to go to a sanitarium. Granddaughter Mary Nichols wrote, "We were watching and waiting for help and Gwendolyn had deteriorated and it was this flu that was the culprit." She died three days after Christmas, 1928. "Grandmother gritted her teeth and went in, and I remember it to this day, tied up her jaw the way they have to do, and then the next morning the ambulance came to take her. They hadn't got the word that she'd passed away."

Gwendolyn's death made an impression on nine-year-old Mary, who remembered that even though Mattie never cried, she could tell that her grandmother "felt dreadful." In typical Mattie fashion, "she was broken-hearted, but she made the best of it as she had always done and just carried on in the family always looking out for us one way or another. ... In spite of the heartache she'd had, she was always good-natured and was always boosting other people up."[15] Mattie must have poured her heart out into her journals. Without them (and in the absence of any correspondence of hers on Gwendolyn's death), it is difficult to gauge the depth of her despair. But Elizabeth wrote, "Although mother made a semblance of living for three more years, her heart was buried with her beloved."[16]

Angus died on June 7, 1915, aged eighty-one. Four of his six wives survived him, Amanda having died in 1905 and Sarah in 1912.

---

15. Nichols, "History of Elizabeth Rachel Cannon Porter McCrimmon."
16. Elizabeth Cannon Porter to Claire Noall, Feb. 13, 1938.

Despite their often-contentious relationship, Angus and Mattie's love for each other is unquestionable. Helen Ovard, Mattie's oldest granddaughter, remembered her mother saying Mattie adored her husband, although she often spoke negatively of him.

By about 1920, Mattie was permanently living in Los Angeles, where all her children had settled, in a home purchased by James. In fact, all of Mattie's adult children lived within a few blocks of each other and her, making a tight little community: no criticism was tolerated. None of the children were particularly "homey"—nor was Mattie herself. Helen Ovard remembers Mattie at this time being "very businesslike," although she did own a pincushion made as the skirt of a porcelain doll, upon which Mattie had embroidered "Helen." Mattie found it convenient to live uphill from James. When his children were, in her opinion, making too much noise, she simply tossed rocks down the hill towards them until they quieted down.[17] Mattie never cooked for herself, so granddaughter Helen took meals up the hill to her.

Mattie kept a tight house. She loved flowers and enjoyed gardening. One photograph, taken some time in the late 1920s, shows her standing next to her luxuriant rhododendron bushes. Her home, which James had built for her behind his own at 4038 North Homer Street, was small, so Mattie did not have to worry about cleaning, which she had always despised. But still fastidious about her appearance, she dressed every morning: brooches, earrings, hairpiece, dress. She had to be nicely groomed and bejeweled: "I'm ready for anything that could come today."[18]

Knowing that her medical skills and knowledge were not current, Mattie did not attempt to get licensed in California; however, she performed volunteer work in areas that were of interest to her, most notably at the Selwyn Emmett Graves Memorial Dispensary, a clinic for the indigent associated with the UCLA medical program, where she helped with those suffering from narcotic addiction.[19] Even though she was going back and forth between the Oasis Ranch

17. Helen Cannon Ovard, interview with the author, Aug. 1988.
18. Peterson, interview; Ovard, interview; Nichols, "History of Elizabeth Rachel Cannon Porter McCrimmon."
19. Blaine Brady (great-great grandson), interview with the author, Nov. 8, 2013, at his home in Spanish Fork, Utah.

and Los Angeles, in 1918 she was listed in the Los Angeles Medical Department Register of the University of California at Berkeley.[20] Typically, she gave the Oasis Ranch as a temporary address and Los Angeles as her permanent residence.

Just before the end of World War I, Mattie received a government appointment to act as a physician overseas during the worldwide flu pandemic that killed over 50 million people. She never served but was proud of her appointment and kept the letter framed in her home.

Mattie got around Los Angeles by streetcar, having never learned to drive. One day, the streetcar she was riding stopped unexpectedly, throwing her. This incident marked the beginning of her final physical decline. Elizabeth wrote: "In 1931, while watching a parade at the Coliseum, Mother became ill. We closed her house and took her up on the hill where she spent the last year of her life. Just after New Year's 1932, an abdominal operation for [colon] cancer was performed on her at the Glendale Sanitarium, with eight surgeons in attendance.[21]

Mary Nichols, Mattie's granddaughter, reported that her grandmother's last illness gradually wore Elizabeth down. One day, twelve-year-old Mary went to the sanitarium in Eagle Rock, near Los Angeles, to visit Mattie. Upon arriving, she was startled to see Mattie so ill and began to cry, realizing that her grandmother would never be coming home. Mary recalled in an oral interview that when she burst into tears, Mattie told her, "'Mary, go over there and dry your eyes; straighten up.' [In the interview, Mary laughed.] She didn't say straighten up, but that's what she meant: 'Just make the best of it.' You know she didn't [actually] say that but 'blow your nose and dry your eyes.'" With her flinty spirit honed by years of adversity, Mattie told her granddaughter, "You go into the corner and wash your face. There will be no tears here."[22]

Mattie passed away on July 10, 1932, age seventy-five, of complications following surgery for colon cancer.[23] Obituaries appeared

20. *Los Angeles Medical Department Register* (Berkeley, CA: University of California, Berkeley, 1918), 163.

21. Elizabeth Cannon Porter to Claire Noall, Feb. 13, 1938.

22. Mary Nichols, interview with Nancy Green, KUED, 2012; typescript in my possession.

23. Mattie's official death certificate specifies the cause of death as "carcinoma of rectum with metastases" with contributing factors of "general toxicosis associated with malignancy."

in newspapers across the nation, most of them heralding her as the first woman state senator. "Early Woman Senator Dies: Dr. Martha Hughes Cannon, ex-Utah Lawmaker," wrote the *Los Angeles Times,* noting that she had lived in Los Angeles for the last twelve years of her life. *The New York Times* declared, "Dr. Martha H. Cannon: Physician of Utah and First Woman to Serve in State Senate;" and the *Chicago Daily Tribune* noted that the "1st Woman State Senator Die[d] in Los Angeles at 75."[24]

Elizabeth commented dryly, "Mother, who didn't believe in funerals, had two. The first [held at the Reed Brothers, Tapley & Geiger Mortuary] was in Los Angeles, largely attended by James' employees. The Apostle Rudger Clawson was the speaker."[25]

The second funeral was held on July 14, 1932, in Salt Lake City in the Tenth Ward chapel, where Mattie attended church as a child. Alice Merrill Horne, who had served with Mattie in the Utah Legislature, spoke of her first as a friend, "who was older than I and was wise. ... We stand before the bier of a friend ... in whose life we read of study and travel and achievement, a leader among women." Horne reminisced on their work together: "I saw her moving in the circles with the forward-looking women of Zion. ... I met her in the Third Legislature of Utah in 1899, a competent person, a just legislator, a parliamentarian, a gracious, kindly, beautiful woman, a lover of good. Men and women took counsel from her."[26]

Within her own family, familiarity with Mattie's life and achievements was not uniform. She suppressed her own accomplishments so successfully that her oldest granddaughter, Helen Ovard, James's daughter (a teenager when Mattie died), had no idea that her grandmother had been a state senator. She was disappointed when she found out only after reading the obituary because she would never be able to talk to Mattie about her experiences. Elizabeth's children

---

24. "Early Woman Senator Dies," *Los Angeles Times,* July 11, 1932; "Dr. Martha Hughes Cannon; Physician of Utah and First Woman to Serve in State Senate," *New York Times,* July 11, 1932, 13; "1st Woman State Senator Dies in Los Angeles at 75," *Chicago Daily Tribune,* July 11, 1932, 12.

25. Elizabeth Cannon Porter to Claire Noall, Feb. 13, 1938; Ober, "History of Elizabeth Rachel Cannon Porter McCrimmon," 31–32.

26. Typescript copy of Horne's talk in my possession.

and grandchildren knew all the stories of Mattie's life as fashioned by Elizabeth, but James's children were not as well-informed.[27]

By the time Mattie died, she had been largely forgotten by Salt Lake City, the LDS Church, and the Utah newspapers that had previously breathlessly detailed her activities. After her death, a flurry of publications released sketches of Mattie's life, most fueled by Elizabeth's desire for her mother to be recognized by history. All the articles were slavishly complimentary, and falsehoods and romantic fabrications were already creeping into the record.

Even during her lifetime, inaccuracies were springing up. In 1913, the *Macon Daily Telegraph* printed a short article in which Mattie was depicted as a woman who still took "great interest in public affairs, and who had been particularly interested in [and probably incensed] by newspaper accounts in which the honor of first becoming a woman state senator was accredited to Mrs. Helen Ring Robinson, of Colorado."[28]

More recent events have conspired to make Mattie's memory hazy. At the corner of 200 West and South Temple, near where her old home and office once stood in Salt Lake City, there is a monument whose inscription reads: "In memory of Dr. Martha Hughes Cannon—pioneer doctor—first woman state senator in U.S.—author of Utah sanitation laws—member of first state board of health." Mattie deserves such a monument. However, it has a cracked and stained concrete base placed with its blank backside facing South Temple and the inscribed side facing an empty lot. Its design is so uninspiring as to recall a utility box.

Perhaps it is inevitable that inaccuracies creep into written histories, but some of the mistakes are howlers, based on little to no research. For example, in the May/June 2012 issue of a popular lifestyle magazine, *LDS Living*, readers were told that Angus was also a physician.[29]

At least one researcher has speculated that Mattie's testimony of the LDS Church was shaky, and that she struggled with her faith.[30]

27. Ovard, interview; Arline Brady, interview with the author, Feb. 2, 2012.
28. "First Woman to Sit in a Senate Seat," *Macon Daily Telegraph*, Dec. 27, 1913.
29. "Mormon Firsts," *LDS Living*, May/June 2012, 38.
30. Telephone conversation, 2019; identity of caller kept private.

Nothing could be further from the truth. Yes, in several of her exile letters she rails against polygamy. But to her dying day she said she believed in it. It was the way she was forced to live it, at the height of the persecutions against the polygamists, that she hated. She often taught Sunday school, where she remarked that if she could just struggle through, she knew God would help her. On Sundays, she often bore eloquent testimony of her faith. Helen Ovard recalls being embarrassed and slinking down in the pew because of Mattie's display of emotion as she spoke, her testimony given in the ringing tones she had learned so long ago at the National School in Philadelphia.[31]

In recent years, Mattie has been featured in the news. In 1995 a Martha Hughes Cannon Room was dedicated in the Salt Lake City–County Building. The Martha Hughes Cannon Health Building in Salt Lake City was dedicated on June 12, 1986, honoring Mattie as an outspoken advocate for public health.

In early 2020, a statue of Mattie was to be unveiled in the US Capitol's National Statuary Hall, replacing the statue of Philo T. Farnsworth, inventor of the television. Her statue "champions Utah and the West's role in the suffrage movement and commemorates the anniversary of the 19th Amendment."[32] The COVID pandemic has delayed its installation, however.

Mattie's star is rising once more. But why did her memory lapse into obscurity? It was probably because she made it so easy. Though living on a very public stage, she was an intensely private person. She admonished Angus (and other correspondents) to burn everything she wrote, once chastising Angus when she found out he had left some of her notes on his desk where anyone could read them. An excerpt from a letter to her husband may explain why she did not want others reading her letters and, ultimately, gives us a clue as to why she wanted her journals and papers burned after her death. Despite the ups and down of their relationship, Angus remained her confidant, whom she trusted with her most intimate thoughts. After an exchange from England where she had waxed eloquent about her disdain for Emmeline B. Wells, she wrote that she had never

---

31. Ovard, interview.
32. Lisa Christensen, "Utah Votes to Send Martha Hughes Cannon Statue to U.S. Capitol's National Statuary Hall in 2020," *Utah Business*, Feb. 19, 2018.

expressed such feelings to anyone but to him. In still another letter, she admonished him to say nothing to Romania's husband about Mattie's opinion of Emmeline "as of a surety [it] will be rehearsed to the Dr. [Romania]—something that I don't feel inclined to tolerate."[33] Her personal journals and writings were certainly full of similar criticisms that she would not have wanted circulated.

It is fitting to allow those who loved and knew her best—her family—to offer their epitaphs on their mother, grandmother, and great-grandmother.

Elizabeth wrote, "She was not only our mother, but our best friend. We liked to talk together, and go to the same places. She was a Rock of Gibraltar to whom all of her family carried their troubles. The waves might dash against her but it did not faze her strength. Her patience and wisdom never failed us."[34]

Granddaughter Mary Nichols remembered Mattie's ability to keep going. When asked what some of Mattie's greatest attributes were, Mary said, "To forge ahead—just to keep forging ahead and making the best of whatever you had to manage." And, "if she got an idea in her head, she pretty much went ahead with it, you know, and she wasn't deterred very easily." Mary's father died when she was only two months old, so Mattie helped rear her: "Grandma Cannon was the constant in my life and we enjoyed walks and reading and talking about life. She was very wise and advised me well as I was growing up."[35]

Great-granddaughter Joanne Peterson described her as a "marvelous woman, but different—hard to live with—but all worshipped her."[36]

Mattie herself wrote in 1887 (of her English exile, though the thought applies just as easily to her life as a whole): "I feel now that the keenness of the ordeal is passed—and so far as I am concerned, it will remain an untold tale. [I am] satisfied with the fact that God

33. Constance L. Lieber and John Sillito, eds., *Letters from Exile: The Correspondence of Martha Hughes Cannon and Angus M. Cannon, 1886–1888* (Salt Lake City: Signature Books, 1989), 9, 30, 34, and 74.

34. Mary Idelia Porter Ober Nichols, "Molly O: My Life Story," 51, copy in my possession.

35. Nichols, "Molly O: My Life Story," 51.

36. Petersen, interview.

knows all about it—and myself none the worse for the experience I have had."[37]

Happily, the joys, accomplishments, disappointments, and ordeals that define the life of Martha Hughes Cannon are no longer an "untold tale."

---

37. Lieber and Sillito, *Letters from Exile*, 190.

POSTSCRIPT

Over eighty years after Mattie's death, I sat reading a book that had belonged to her. I held it, treasuring the thought that Mattie had once had it in her own hands. That might have been enough—but then I noticed the few faint penciled quotation marks inserted into the text with the name "Gwendolyn" written next to those passages—and I realized I was holding what might be the only extant proof of Mattie's grief at her daughter's passing. She noted the following passage:

> Her portrait I'll paint you,
> But that will acquaint you
> With only the least of her charms;
> Though her loveliness dare
> With perfection compare,
> And her sweetness all censure disarms.

Oh, Gwendolyn! What a lovely picture of a lost daughter. Another marked passage bears proof of Mattie's intense emotion and depression over her daughter's death: "Ay the sadness born of darkness."

The final marked section reflects both Mattie's love for Gwendolyn and her faith that she would see her daughter again. The parting may be long, but it is not final.

> Good night! And oh!—a long good bye,
> Thou darling of my heart![1]

---

1. Orson F. Whitney (1855–1931), "Love and the Light: An Idyl of the Westland," published by Orson F. Whitney in Salt Lake City, 1918. The cited selections are on pp. 25, 60, 92. Whitney wrote what Mattie must have felt as she read his poem: "Poetry is that sentiment of the soul, or faculty of the mind, which enables its possessor to appreciate and realize the heights and depths of human experience. It is the power to feel pleasure or suffer pain in all its exquisiteness and intensity" (*Woman's Exponent*, Nov. 1, 1886, 82).

Now I am sitting at my computer, trying to think of a way to sum up a life that was groundbreaking and astonishing—but also, like most lives, prosaic and quotidian. I think that, above all, it is important to examine Mattie in the context of her times. Today, amid the renewed excitement about—almost the re-discovery of—Martha Hughes Cannon, many are too anxious to make her a woman of *our* time. "Let's emphasize her dependence on drugs to make her more relatable to those who struggle with addiction!" "Let's examine her wavering faith in the LDS Church to help those who struggle with their own faith see a commonality!" It would be doing her a disservice to categorize her use of drugs to ease the discomfort of congestive heart failure as dependence or even addiction. We know those drugs were ineffective and even dangerous in the doses she used, but the medicine of her time did not teach that. Her letters to Angus railing against polygamy did not signify a lost faith in that system, but rather discouragement and even anger about how she was forced to live it. But perhaps even more dangerous than those enthusiasms, based on a skewed reading of her letters, is our desire to make her more than she was.

She was a female physician, but that was not, even in her day, a singular accomplishment. She was one of many women doctors who were members of the LDS Church. What she did was step out of the norm when it came to medical education for women, seeking the best, most comprehensive education she could get and demonstrating to her contemporaries that they could compete with and meet men on common ground. She attended the University of Michigan Medical School, as one of the first female students at a time when the educating of future male and female physicians was still partially segregated. She did that rather than attend one of the women's medical schools, which her contemporaries in Utah had done, convinced that she would receive a more rigorous medical training there. She supplemented that with further training at the medical school of the University of Pennsylvania (the only woman in her class) and enhanced her ability to articulate her thoughts by attending the National School of Elocution and Oratory. She may not have been the best physician among her peers, but she was the one people turned to because she could be trusted to ensure their general, not just

physical, well-being. That was evident in one of her reasons for going into exile in 1886—to avoid being put into the position of being
"the proof" of polygamous unions and thereby sending polygamous
fathers to prison. Her level-headed assessment of her declining medical skills, which prompted her to give up private medical practice,
demonstrates integrity. Meanwhile, her continued volunteer work in
the medical field speaks to her dedication to her chosen profession.

One wonders what those who had been fighting for woman
suffrage for so long thought when Mattie burst upon the scene.
She hailed from a state only recently liberated (as the larger public understood it) from the scourge of polygamy, where women
were considered to be their husbands' pawns. But not only did she
demonstrate that LDS women were independent, forward-thinking,
and modern, she also demonstrated her enthusiasm for suffrage by
being the first woman in the state to be registered to vote. And then
she went on to win political office, defeating (among others) her
own husband.

Mattie did this her whole life: taking two clashing ideologies
(e.g., polygamy and suffrage) and finding a way to make them work.
Perhaps that is her greatest accomplishment: she was able, for most
of her life, to force doors to open and contradictions to coexist, thus
helping modify and influence public opinion in ways that many of
her contemporaries had not considered.

In the end, Mattie's is the story of a fun-loving, determined,
brave soul caught amid church teachings, Victorian mores, and the
changing role of women—between worldly and familial success. In
1899, her romantic vision of having another child in a polygamous
relationship collided with the realities of being a woman in her political position— but this time they could not coexist. Certainly,
she attained a large measure of happiness within the circle of her
children and grandchildren. But as Annie Laurie told her when she
was elected senator, she marked the beginning of great things for
women—and was only partially able to live up to that potential. Yet
her family says she remained fiercely loyal to the other promises she
made: to her church, to her husband, to her children.

We must not couch her life in terms of right or wrong decisions.
That would be imposing our time-bound opinions upon her. I look

back at her with admiration because she took on her challenges and, right or wrong, made decisions and forged ahead over the course of a remarkable life.

It is the biographer's task to pick and choose among the facts and stories of a life, opting to include what seem to be the most vital, the most characteristic, details. I have tried to write using D. Michael Quinn's insight as a guide: "History is what we are able to discover of the past; historical fantasy is what we wish had occurred."[2] In relating and summing up Mattie's journey, I have attempted to be true to the historical record (as much as can be discovered of it in Mattie's case) and to steer clear of the romanticized versions that found their way into print in the first decades following her death. Mattie's life, unembellished, is fantastic enough.

---

2. D. Michael Quinn, "LDS Church Authority and New Plural Marriages, 1890–1904," *Dialogue: A Journal of Mormon Thought* 18, no. 1 (Spring 1985): 105.

INDEX

Ballmer, Anna, 30–31

Cannon, Angus Munn, xi; death, 92; state senate campaign, 53–56; trial (1885), 26–28; release from prison, 29

Cannon, Angus Munn Jr., 26

Cannon, Elizabeth Rachel, ix; illness, 35–36, 37, 38; wedding, 89; death of husband, 90

Cannon, Gwendolyn, 91–92, 101

Cannon, Martha Hughes xi–xii, 1; Algonac, Michigan (1887), 34–35; Angus 1885 trial, 26, 27, 28; Ann Arbor, Michigan (1887), 35; Annie Laurie interview, 59–61; birth of Gwendolyn and press coverage, 72–75, 76; in California 80, 85, 91, 93; in Canada with Angus, 34; Columbian Exposition (1893), 48–49; confidence as a physician, 83–84; courtship and marriage, 23–25; depression, 33–34; Deseret Hospital, 20–22; England, ix; exile to England, 30, 34; exile to San Francisco, 42–43; final illness and death, 94–95; home in Salt Lake City, 40, 43–44; illness, 36–37, 76, 81, 86, 87–89, 90; jealousy, 31–33; legacy, 95–97, 102–104; marital problems, 68–69, 77, 80, 82; medical practice in Michigan, 19–20; medical practice in Salt Lake City, 27, 40, 41, 44, 49, 78, 93, 94; medical school, 18–20; medical school in Michigan 15–18; National School (Philadelphia), 20–21; nursing school, 41; politics after 1899, 78, 79, 80–81, 91; pregnancies, 27, 71; pre-medical school, 10–13; private life, 68, 76–77, 83; San Francisco earthquake, 86; state senator, 53–62; views: on classes of women 46–47; on political office for women, 48; on polygamy, 28, 31; on suffrage, 45, 46–48, 49–51; voting for US Senator (1887), 66–67; voting for US Senator (1899), 67–68

Deseret Hospital, 20–22

Evans, Elizabeth, 1, 9–10

Horne, Alice Merrill, on Martha Hughes Cannon, 63

Hughes, Martha Maria. *See* Cannon, Martha Hughes

Hughes Family immigration, 2–9

Mormon Underground, 29

105